To: Ko
You in
some

MW00760465

The Dog Ate My Budget

Tales About Teaching and Managing in the Ivy Tower

Ross A. Webber

Professor Emeritus, The Wharton School
University of Pennsylvania
Drawings by Andrew R. DePietro

Copyright © 2008 Ross A. Webber
All rights reserved.

ISBN: 1-4392-0648-1
ISBN-13: 9781439206485
Library of Congress Control Number: 2008907314

Visit www.booksurge.com to order additional copies.

TO

Heather Margaret Webber Bannister
Hillary Elyse Burton Bannister
Meredith Sarah DePietro
Andrew Ronald DePietro
Jillian Claire Foradora Bannister
Meghan Jane Stevens Bannister
Victoria Llywelyn Arkell Bannister
Christian William DePietro
Tristan Trevor William Bannister
Kaethe Louise Walther
Sullivan Michael Webber
Hardy Noble Walther
Rory McLaughlin Webber
Emily Hearne Walther
Eleanor Carroll Webber
Jack Frederick Webber
Ceclia Scout Webber

Past, Present and Future University Students

Table of Contents

Preface
A Doctoral Thesis is Waxed

I wrote my doctoral dissertation the old fashioned way – on a manual portable typewriter encompassing many drafts. By the time I reached the final, final version, I was typed out. So I hired a professional typist at what seemed to a then poverty stricken graduate student as an exorbitant page rate.

With impatience I awaited the final manuscript so I could submit it to Columbia University and justify my already teaching at the University of Pennsylvania. When my expert typist never called, I telephoned her. The tone of her voice suggested trouble. With embarrassment she explained that she had spilled a can of floor wax on my typed manuscript. It now had the consistency of a brick – perhaps useful as a door stop. She had tried to heat the brick to melt the wax, but …….sorry.

I should have known right then that my life in academia would be filled with strange events. And it was. Collected in this book are some of the humorous adventures and ironic misadventures that I have experienced. Of course not all seemed funny at the time. On many I was reminded of Adlai Stevenson's retelling of a Lincoln lament at the time of his second presidential election loss: "It hurts too much to laugh, but I'm too old to cry." Time, however, lessens the pain and increases the absurdity. All of these tales are true – or at least the descriptions are consistent with my perception of what transpired.

The tales describe incidents involving students, faculty, alumni and the outside world. I have disguised the identities of all the students and faculty mentioned. I do name those alumni and university administrators whom I admire. I apologize to anyone who feels offended or embarrassed by my possibly faulty memory of incidents in which they think they were involved.

Few institutions are as complex as large research universities. From the simplest freshman survey course to the management of a multi-billion dollar budget, almost everything will play out other than as planned. To survive for a significant period of time, complexity and unpredictability demand a tolerance for ambiguity and a sense of humor. I hope you will find both in this collection of tales.

I am grateful to Susan Mosher Stuard, Emeritus Professor of History at Haverford College for providing the initial spark for writing this book. I am indebted to Sarah DePietro for giving me the ever present notebook in which I recorded all my memories of academia. Judith Webber helped enormously with editing and other suggestions. Finally I am in debt to many University of Pennsylvania leaders who helped me at various times across forty years: William Gomberg, Vartan Gregorian, Sheldon Hackney, Martin Meyerson, Herbert Northrup,

Edward Shils, Rita Tomassone, Helen Wright and Willis Wynn. Special thanks to Barbara Corsi, Donna DeBuonaventura and Renee Newstein who were my secretaries when I was The Wharton School's Chairman of the Management Department and Penn's Vice President for Development and University Relations.

Most of all I am thankful that my wife Mary Louise Foradora Webber shared in these adventures as they occurred or heard my later lamentations.

– Ross A. Webber,
Haddonfield, N.J. 2008

I. Teaching

The Pilfered Text Books

"Congratulations, Professor Webber!" So exclaimed the telephone voice of the University Librarian. "All the copies of your book *Becoming a Courageous Manager* have been stolen."

To save students from having to buy another expensive book, I had placed multiple copies of my book on reserve so that students could read it in the library. Most of my course readings were in a reproduced course pack that students purchase but some books I placed on reserve and requested that the University Book Store have them available for sale. On one hand, as an author I could interpret this book disappearance as flattering. Obviously, students were going to the library and reading the book. On the other hand, if they liked it so much why didn't they purchase it at the bookstore? Not a single copy had been sold to a student.

The assigned reading was about the courage needed to maintain personal ethical behavior when it isn't reinforced by the group or organization in which you work. It even included data I had collected that showed that business school students had markedly lower personal ethics than mid- and senior-level executives – a proposal that the students loudly opposed in class discussion.

Investigation revealed that the missing books had not actually been removed from the building. Rather, individual students had miss-shelved them in unique locations known only to them so they could easily be retrieved when wanted again.

How ironic that one of my dusty *Courageous Manager* books may still be residing on the shelves of Lippincott Library next to an expose of the ENRON scandal. Other copies seem to have disappeared like the ark in Spielberg's film "*Raiders of the Lost Ark*" into an infinitely cavernous warehouse.

An Impolitic Student

I pulled my flaming orange FIAT Spider roadster into the parking lot and hastened to an advising session for incoming MBA students. I was to advise them on courses to take as well as evaluate their petitions for waivers of required courses based on prior academic work and experience. One new student who had watched me pull into the parking lot complemented me on my car, but then observed, "You seem to be too old for it." Out of the mouth of babes may indeed come truth, but that was not one that I wanted to hear.

To compound his plea for a course waiver of the required course in organizational behavior and management, in response to my question of "why", he said that he had heard that it was "bullshit." He argued that it would be "irrelevant." to his proposed major in Finance. Worst of all, he was oblivious to the fact that I was the chief designer and course director. I didn't approve his waiver request, but did ensure that he wasn't enrolled in my section.

Such interpersonal ineptitude is not rare among high achieving MBA students. I once asked a major recruiter how graduates fared at her firm. She replied that they all are very hard working, but that perhaps half of them left by mutual agreement in two or three years. When asked why, she said that they tend to see people as items in an algorithmic formula rather than as human beings. Like many young professionals high in achievement need (e.g., MBA, LLD and MD candidates), they often see others as impersonal tools or instruments rather than as colleagues.

The undergraduate engineers among our MBA students frequently voice their distaste for organizational "politics." They want their brains and accomplishments to be the sole determinant of their status and rewards. Yet, I would argue that to be human in any institution demands that you be involved in its politics. As Rollo May warned us in *Power and Innocence* at the height of the 1970's anti-authority and don't trust anyone over thirty era, to reject contending for power is not innocence, but acquiescence.

What was especially galling about my young petitioner's stance was that, like the majority of our students he intended to major in Finance (rather than my field of Human Resource Management).

Perhaps he ended up heading The World Bank.

The Case of the Diaphanous Blouse

Theresa came early to the first class and sat in the front row – a little odd since most students, hoping to escape the professor's attention, choose to fill the seats from the rear forward. Since I didn't assign seats I gave them a chance to move if they preferred. Theresa remained firmly in front of me. If she wanted my attention, she got it in spades.

More precisely, what attracted my attention was the exceedingly sheer blouse that she usually wore, along with what lay beneath. Although I an no more of an expert of this topic than any other heterosexual male, Theresa had the most beautiful breasts I had ever seen – even if a bit fuzzy behind the gauze of her blouse. Too melon-like to be called perky, but still without the apparent aid of support, gravity defying. When she would raise an arm to brush back her honey blond hair, it was easy for me to lose track of the organizational behavior theories that I was trying to impart.

Was she making a pass at me? It was the early 1970's, sexual liberation was in the air and I was not that much older (probably 38 to her 20). Alas, I was of that 1950's generation that believed that one married right out of college and thereafter remained faithful. Yes, I was a square, but this undoubtedly saved me from a career and life disaster. It is hard to be fired from a tenured professorship, but an affair with an undergraduate in one's class would pass the hurdle of "moral turpitude".

Or was it a power move? Feminism was on the march, so perhaps she wanted to demonstrate that a beautiful girl could be smarter than the teacher. And in fact, she was. Years later, I was reminded of Theresa's brilliance when I saw the scene in the film "*Good Will Hunting*" where the MIT math professor grovels on the floor to pick up the torn pieces of the young janitor's term paper. Matt Damon's creativity was so superior to anything that the Professor has ever produced.

So it was with Theresa. Her papers read like she had climbed inside my head and gave everything a more creative turn than I could. I described Abraham Maslow's human need hierarchy as, "A developmental model of maturation showing how an individual climbs up a ladder from being primarily motivated by dependence on others through craving their love and esteem up to the more mature needs seeking personal achievement and self-actualization". In contrast, Theresa wrote: "Maslow's need hierarchy is a downward spiral akin to Dante's Inferno on which human beings progress from the care and love of others to the self-absorption and loneliness of power and isolation."

Needless to say, she earned an A in the course and graduated to a position with a leading management-consulting firm. Years later, when I was a guest speaker at the Boston Alumni Club I met her again. She was still lovely and sexy – and accompanied by her female partner, affirming that my self-control so many years before saved me from at least a severe blow to my self-illusion of irresistibility.

The Massacred Trees

An unexpected result of the personal computer's arrival into academia was the enormous increase in the pieces of paper handed out in class. One or two page mimeographed lecture outlines had been the norm. Students would augment these sketchy handouts with scribbled marginal notes or, for the more ambitious, legible handwriting in a notebook. Unhappily, instruction in cursive handwriting has been eliminated from most U.S. primary schools and the bulk of today's student can write only laboriously in block printing using an awkwardly clenched hand that aches after a couple of pages. Microsoft PowerPoint changed all that.

Professors now can develop lovely full color computer projected overheads that dramatically increase the density and efficiency of the ideas to be communicated in a fifty-minute class. Indeed the medium's greatest contribution is demanding that the teacher more clearly understand and organize his or her material. Teaching quality has improved. The increased pace, however, creates an assimilation problem, so students demand personal copies of every overhead so that their note taking is minimized.

Maximized, however, is the paper load. Even fitting three or four overheads on a single page can result in ten to fifteen page handouts for every student. With three classes of 65 students each, I would be carrying upwards of twenty-nine hundred 8.5 by 11 inch pages of paper to the day's first class. So much for the paperless classroom.

Of course, a well-prepared teacher could distribute the overheads in advance to the students via the internet. This would save the professor's back and even save school money by shifting the printing ink and paper charges to the students thereby adding to their post-graduation debt.

Reading Newspapers in Class

Many graduate business school faculty in recent years have complained about the lessening of student "engagement." Or as my then high school daughter Judy asked after visiting my university class, "Dad, I enjoyed the class, but why were those students reading the newspaper during your lecture?"

In my own case, student disinterest was reflected in a sharp reduction in my teaching ratings. They just no longer seemed interested in what I had to say about human motivation and leadership. They were impatient and frustrated by the reality that I couldn't give them bottom line answers to the perplexing problems raised by human beings in organizations. I wanted words; they preferred numbers.

All my work assignments and tests were open book case and topic reports about ambiguous problems. Most students preferred analytical quantitative tools that could produce an immediate payoff financially. Such skills are of course important and rightly rewarded in early corporate positions. But succeeding in more senior management requires integration of the various functions along with the ability to conceptualize different questions and possibilities. And this was what I was trying to impart.

Nonetheless, difficult as it is to admit, too many students responded to my classes in management with an observation that I advanced too many theories when managing people is just "common sense." Because human behavior is difficult to quantify, some pragmatists see any theory construction as suspect. But even the most hardheaded pragmatist has his or her theories about people – particularly how money is supposed to motivate them. My job was to help them clarify their own theories and to test them against the evidence of theirs and others' experience. In fact, nothing is as practical as a workable theory because it helps you cut through the confusion of apparently random events. Some people work twenty years but only repeat the same experience twenty times. Building personal theories ensures that you ask of self and others questions that will create twenty years of new experiences.

When Wharton was introducing its new graduate curriculum, we convened a meeting of alumni, executives, and eminent scholars to give us feedback on the challenges we were confronting. The executives urged us to persist in pushing our students to develop their interpersonal skills and ambiguity tolerance. And Peter Drucker observed, "Seldom have I seen a successful institution put itself through more agony in an effort to improve itself." I took that as a compliment.

Barbara Chester on the Casting Couch

Our curriculum recasting was a response to the desire of hiring firms for graduates more adept at interpersonal relations and better able to handle ambiguous tasks. In a small number of first year cohorts, we experimented with novel educational approaches. I worked with two sections of sixty students each in a required course in teamwork and leadership. Knowing how valuable seeing oneself in a video can be for gaining insight into one's behavior, I decided to have every student do something that could be filmed.

Remembering my own short-lived acting experience and how intense rehearsals can be, I adapted some of my written cases into short plays, which student teams could rehearse and then show to their classmates for discussion. One of these plays consisted of interviews with four candidates for the presidency of a medium sized manufacturing company. Candidate A was the Finance VP, B the VP of Marketing, C the production VP, and D the VP for engineering and research. The class would rank the candidates in desirability. A was usually last because he was seen as an obsolete authoritarian; B generally ranked low as a somewhat shallow salesperson type. The competition was between C and D, who were both seen as strong but with some weaknesses,

To test for discrimination, I would cast C (Chester) with a female. This had no negative affect on C's rating by either men or women. I then would vary being a heavy smoker or being sharply overweight between C and D. Smoking or weight had no effect on the rating of a male D; being overweight, however dramatically reduced Barbara Chester's rating. Being fat reduces promotability, especially for women.

The critical attribute in comparing C and D was who was seen as being more approachable and willing to listen to a subordinate's ideas. The students projected themselves into the case and imagined which candidate they would prefer to work for. These insights were especially dramatic during rehearsal when the actors wanted to rewrite their lines to make their character more sympathetic. But the most powerful learning occurred when the actors responded to classmates' comments and questions. Having to give extemporaneous answers demanded that they understood their character. Some actors playing the authoritarian Finance VP and the playboy Marketing VP even came to prefer them.

Some students complained about my emphasis on role-playing. When asked why I did it, I would explain that learning is more powerful when one is under some stress. Few situations more effectively produce this stress than having to think and talk spontaneously to a class of peers – and then see in a video how well or badly you did.

No One Ever Cheated ın My Class!

Allow me some poetic license here, but I am confident that cheating in my classes was appreciably less than recent collegiate scandals would suggest. My students certainly were not more ethical than those at Duke or the Air Force Academy. Rather, I simply gave them less opportunity. As I read of those unhappy events, I was disappointed in the students but also angry at the naive faculty that created conditions facilitating cheating, including multiple-choice questions and timed window "closed book" tests.

Most of my exams were open book. In class, they were allowed to consult whatever materials they had brought with them. Indeed the process of deciding what to bring and organizing it is a wonderful study process. They were not allowed to talk to each other which I monitored by staying in the room (happily, text messaging had not yet reared its ugly head). On course papers, I encouraged them to talk with whomever they chose – another judgment conducive to thinking about the material. Key is to make these tests unique to each student by requiring them to write about something in their own life or work experience. Using course theories and concepts, they were to analyze some past or current situation.

Of course, some students complained that they had so little experience that they could find nothing to write about. I would suggest that they were at least 20 years old and that they must have had some relevant experiences albeit it social fraternities or athletic teams. Nonetheless, if still stumped, they could analyze someone else's experience, especially their parents – a great device for putting some in touch with a parent's career. In later years, I had them make PowerPoint oral presentations in class about these analyses. There is no learning like teaching. And I got to sit in the back and bug the teacher.

Of course, I can't guarantee that some of these experiences and analysis weren't fabricated. But even if they were fictitious, plausibility would have been a good indicator of the student's mastery. What was next to impossible, however, was copying a classmate's paper. Even with a large pile of papers that I would read sometimes groggily in bed, duplication would be obvious.

But my approach to discouraging cheating was a lot of work!

Your Face or Mine?

Like death and taxes, giving grades will always be with us. Some schools have tried to downplay the importance of grades by shifting to Pass-Fail systems, or allowing students to take a portion of classes for "Non-Credit." Some radical faculty try to defeat the system by giving all their students "A's." But pressure from prospective employers and graduate schools along with the perceived necessity to motivate students impels traditional grading to return. Some schools have even returned to forced grading distributions.

Nonetheless, the social dynamics of grading and faculty-student relations have changed. To protect student identities and avoid embarrassing them, grades must be given confidentially. They may not be publicly posted by name, social security number or any number that would identify the grade to other students. Graded papers cannot be left in a publicly assessable box for students to retrieve. Only sealed envelopes are acceptable. Semester grades are not even sent to parents; only to the student – reflecting the myth that the student is an adult paying for his or her own tuition.

All of this is intended to protect the student from embarrassment or losing "face" in front of peers. Some students are even protesting cold calls in class that may demonstrate they haven't done the assigned reading.

Others complain that Socratic interaction between teacher and student is unfair to those who are not aggressive in oral argument…All to save face.

How different it is with the treatment of faculty. At the end of every course, students complete questionnaires that rate their teacher on multiple dimensions including whether he/she is prepared, interested in the topic and stimulating. These grades are posted publicly by name and in order of student popularity. Teaching ratings are required in the faculty's dossier for promotion consideration. And they play a major role in influencing whether students enroll in a teacher's elective course, which can affect whether the teacher in the future has a job.

Today's students want to avoid any loss of face from a teacher, but they also want a teacher who is not embarrassed by their complaints. They particularly value professors who are calm in class, never betraying their anger with ill-prepared students or stupid questions. Most of all, students resent a teacher who loses his/her self-control implying retaliation for something said in class.

Thankfully, students still value a professor's preparation, passion about the topic and commitment to teaching, but doing it well is trickier than ever.

Sex Starved MBA Students

For many years I would address Wharton's incoming MBA students on the challenges they would soon confront. Most of them had been outstanding college students with three to five years of work success. At Wharton, however, they could expect to share some disappointing grades as well as negative feedback that might batter their self-illusions of excellence. For most this was a certainly since the school had a forced grading distribution so that less than 20% would receive A's and more than 50% would receive the equivalent of C's. To soften the blow we used a grading scale of "distinguished," "high pass," "pass," and "no credit." But everyone recognized the "pass" as a C.

In addition, the program included a major component of teamwork designed to assist students in developing their interpersonal and leadership skills. This included some brutally honest feedback from their teammates about each individual's contribution to the team projects. A student's grade in some courses could be affected by his or her teammates' judgments of their performance.

Now my wife tells me that the grading distribution (and the possible teammate blackballs) is unfair. Not a few students agreed with her. So after delivering this message I tried to boost their spirits with a report by the

Northwestern Medical School on the marital and sexual satisfaction of various professional degree holders. It seems that more than MD's, LLD's, or PhD's, MBA's have the HIGHEST satisfaction with their sex lives. Now that is a result that makes Wharton's misery worthwhile.

However, I had to warn them that the Dean recommended that this should occur only AFTER graduation, not before.

The Class Casanova

He was a twenty-year-old student in an undergraduate course in organizational psychology. As in most classes, I required students to analyze personal experiences and write a case analyzing their own and others' behavior utilizing course concepts. He wrote an excellent report emphasizing motivation and influence theories. The problem? The report was about all the girls he had seduced.

In (too) great detail, he described his tactics from approach, flattery, and hook-up with a number of his fellow university students. His ability to present himself as a modern metro sexual sensitive and caring male was impressive. He handed in the report with no sense of embarrassment or even awareness that I might have some qualms about it. He was proud of his report, not to mention the behavior therein described.

What was I to do? I couldn't tell whether his story was fiction. And if so, he certainly demonstrated competence in the use of course concepts. If fiction, he might have published it in *Playboy*. If the report depicted actual events, his behavior ran counter to my moral beliefs and, I believe, counter to society's interests. To me the student culture of temporary hook-ups, of sex without love or even romance is repulsive. The deterioration of the campus culture for women over the years has been deeply disturbing. Co-ed housing has contributed to the women's quality of life falling down to the men's.

But what did I know. I was a then 50ish man who had attended an all-male college, still an angry father responding to my undergraduate freshman daughter's dorm room sink being torn out of her wall by a drunken male classmate. I certainly couldn't blame this young student for the mistakes college administrators and students were busily making. Most of the girls and women on campus seemed oblivious to the psychological costs falling mainly on them. Perhaps I was just an obsolete old fuddy-duddy.

I certainly didn't think I was all that old, but I couldn't fail my class Casanova for his immorality. Yet, I couldn't accept the paper as a description of legitimate behavior. So I simply told him that I couldn't accept the paper because it didn't deal with the kind of organization that I expected. Please write it again.

 Years later when I read Tom Wolfe's novel, *Charlotte Simmons*, it was all too familiar.

The Dangers of Humor

Diversity in organizations certainly contributes to organizational creativity and flexibility. But a teacher's or leader's ability to use humor is significantly curtailed. I would frequently tell a rather lengthy joke about a New Hampshire farmer whose property, because of an earlier improper survey, had been determined to actually be in Vermont. When asked if he wanted to appeal, I would reply in full New England accent: "Well, I don't think I could stand another New Hampshire winter anyway." It used to provoke some laughter, but no longer. A class today is so diverse that half of them don't know anything about U.S. regional accents, and half of the American students don't know where New Hampshire is or what its winters are like.

Increasingly, sports or geographical metaphors become questionable. I heard a professor claim that businesses today were in "continual white water." His allusion was to river kayaking and he meant that market conditions are so turbulent that management can't plan strategically, only respond quickly to changing conditions. But the image meant nothing to the students from the Middle East. North Americans frequently make baseball analogies arguing, for example, that a more cautious business strategy is to try "to hit singles, not go for home runs." The argument in this case is that incremental changes are more appropriate than "betting the farm" (another limited analogy) on major innovations. All of these allusions become more questionable and potentially confusing as classes become more culturally diverse.

Increased sensitivity to perceived ethic, racial or gender aspersions has dramatically reduced the range of acceptable citations. White Anglo Saxon Protestant males are still safe targets. Sometimes one can get away with so-called "blond" jokes, but that's about it.

Sheldon Hackney, former President of Penn, was one of the most effective users of humor that I've observed. He could lessen the tension when a group was faced with a difficult situation and create a sense of shared experience, usually by making himself the butt of a joke (as Abraham Lincoln did). But even here, the most zealous among protesting students took this badly. They interpreted his use of even self deprecation as a belittling of the seriousness of their arguments. They literally had no sense of humor because life was too serious to admit humor. That of course is precisely when it is most needed.

The most effective humor today is not the planned joke. It is the clever retort to an unexpected student comment. For example, to a group of alumni I was describing achievement need and the challenges high achievers want in their work. A silver haired executive in the back of the room interrupted with, "Professor

Webber, that's all nonsense. I never met a man I couldn't motivate with either money or sex! What do you think?"

I could only mutter, "Well, unfortunately, I personally have never had a boss who seriously tried either."

Don't Call Me "Doctor"

A close friend who is an ophthalmologist once asked me why I identified myself as "Mister." and not "Doctor." "Didn't I have a Ph.D.," he asked. To the status conscious medical world, it is essential that the pecking order be clearly defined between physicians, registered nurses, nurses' aids, staff, and patients. In at least the non-medical departments of upper tier universities, "Doctor" and even "Professor" are considered a bit gauche. Mr/Ms or Ross or Beth is preferred.

Several contradictory explanations for this misleading egalitarianism exist. Lessening the status labels may facilitate more student and subordinate outspokenness promoting learning and organizational effectiveness. When I taught in Germany, I was "Herr Doktor Professor:" in Italy, "Signore Dottore Professor," etc. This was very flattering, but hardly conducive to eliciting probing student questions. And indeed, in some cultures the teachers simply don't want such questions. Being on a high pedestal can be protective.

But so can stepping down from the high perch. Having professors/leaders on level ground may lessen the pressure on them by lowering other's expectations of their knowledge and wisdom. We admit that we don't know all the answers; that we are in the learning game together. In my consulting engagements, it was imperative that the client and I shift from expert-student relationship to that of colleagues. One of the surest signs that this was not occurring and that the project would fail is when a client wouldn't shift from addressing me as "Doctor" to "Ross."

This need to escape from the "expert" status became very evident when after seventeen years as a professor, I moved to university vice president. Professorial colleagues asked what it was like to control two hundred people and millions of budget dollars. My somewhat vulgar response was that as a professor I worked alone, but as a university executive, I quickly came to realize that I now had at least a hundred people reporting to me who could screw me any time they wanted.

Of course I could discipline or reward individuals, but my and the organization's success was utterly dependent on their skills, motivation and good will. In turn, they were dependent on my ability to represent their resource needs internally and the university's aspirations externally.

Winning budget battles for my subordinates was as essential as attracting donors to new university endeavors. We were totally interdependent.

An Ambiguous Proposition

It wasn't really a strong test of my character. When she came into my office, closed the door and sat down at my desk, the last thing I expected was a sexual proposition (although I guess I should have wondered about the door closing; most women students prefer to keep it ajar). She was an experienced nurse administrator taking my graduate course in management. We were half way through the semester and her grades were a solid B+ or better. She earnestly explained how seriously she viewed the course and how important doing well was to her. "I will do anything for an A."

My immediate interpretation was a request for me to assign her extra credit work, perhaps an additional paper or two. In my confusion, I made a fumbling show of checking her grades in my course records lamely proclaiming that her work was good and that she had a fine chance of receiving an "A". "But, I really want an A," was the somewhat breathless Marilyn-like response. It became quite clear that the extra assignment my petitioner was seeking involved something different from additional analysis of an organization's ideal span of control.

I like to think that my declining her charms was due to my staunch moral character and love of my wife. Yet, I sometimes wonder if I would have been so strong if she hadn't reminded me of Nurse Mildred Ratched in Kelsey's "*One Flew over the Cuckoo's Nest.*" Now, we will never know because, thankfully, no similar proposition ever again came my way.

Unrequited Love

As far as I know, only one student ever thought he was in love with me. Such parental transference is not uncommon toward psychiatrists, surgeons, and teachers, but certainly rare with management professors. I don't know who he was; he never revealed his name. At the time, my three course sections were bursting with almost seventy per section so I didn't recognize his voice from class. Although I cold called on students (much to their annoyance), it was possible for a shy person to be quite invisible.

My unknown admirer would telephone me to say how much he admired my shirts, ties and suits (it was back in the days when professors so dressed). He loved the collar pin I used instead of the regulation button down shirts. He loved the stories I told about my children in class. Presiding over a large family was a rich source of examples of bad and good management (usually me the former and my wife the latter).

More pertinent to the course he was taking, my admirer demonstrated an eerie identification with my thinking. I had recently published a book on how managers manage their time. Particularly difficult for me was the topic of separating time available to others from time alone. Such separation is critical to escaping the tyranny of the short-run. But isolating oneself, even for short periods, runs counter to subordinates' desire for access and a superior's expectation that one will be always available to his or her demands. After reading the book chapter, my anonymous telephone caller observed that the problem was particularly "Yours, Ross, because you want everyone to like you and you aren't tough enough to say no." Alas, probably true.

Perhaps my caller had missed some family life because he would emphasize how lonely he was. He wanted to meet me somewhere. I was generally agreeable to meeting students in my office or in an eatery on campus, but in this case, to be truthful, I was a bit afraid. So I declined. In time, the class and calls ended. I have sometimes wondered if I could have been more helpful to a clearly miserable young man.

Or was my discretion the better part of valor?

Visiting the Doctor's Home

My wife and I liked to invite to dinner the graduate students in my smaller elective courses. We wanted to offer an opportunity for them and their partners to see that academics were real people with traditional lives. Upon arriving at our home, however, they were often shocked to discover that we had five children, a mother-in-law, and a Golden Retriever living with us. For some it was beyond their comprehension.

The young woman especially were amazed to discover that we had had four children by age twenty-nine, precisely the average age of our guests who uniformly had no children. Perhaps carefully disguising their opinion that we were simple-minded, their amazement did produce some interesting conversation and startling candor. My wife and I had all our children with essentially no planning. Indeed, I was away for the birth of two of them – in the Navy for the first and teaching in New Hampshire for the last. Our guests were adamant that conceiving and birthing for them would not be spontaneous. No mistakes in the heat of passion. Their planning of the month, years and career stage at which to become pregnant were worthy of launching a product marketing campaign.

Surely economic and dual career concerns dictate a more planful approach to having a baby than in the past. The young women want to establish themselves in their careers before considering children. And the young men have sharply increased their aspirations for family involvement. They are deeply desirous of being nurturing fathers involved in their children's lives beyond what my 1950's generation conceived. These mutual concerns explain their postponing the birth of first child – today, to the oldest age in American history. My students seem to be draining the fun and poetry out of becoming parents. It has become such a BIG decision.

You Mean I Can't Lecture Anymore?

I spent a lot of time calling on alumni reporting on campus initiatives and trying to plant seeds for future giving. Older alumni would often ask me what had happened to old Professor X. The cited professor was usually before my time, but I did recognize some of the names. The reason they asked usually involved their memories of the great lectures that he gave. What had generally impressed them were the highly personalized and sometimes outrageous views expressed.

I was reminded of this when after many years in administration I was preparing to return to teaching. I sought the guidance of some of our most highly rated teachers in my field of organizational behavior and management. The first advice was that one can't merely lecture anymore; students don't have the attention span, and will not be so passive in class. I was warned that I might enter my lecture room to find only tape recorders in the seats,

Well, I thought I was a good lecturer, but generally, I utilized cases and a Socratic method of questions, answers, and discussion. Unhappily, our highest rated teacher then explained that students were rejecting this approach because they felt that professors were being manipulative in seeking the "right" answers.

Now I was getting nervous. What was I to do? The answer was Exercises. The role of the teacher seems to have evolved to presenting the students with experiential exercises designed to elicit self-learning. That is, from the exercises or games they intuit the managerial lesson. The teacher acts as a discussion leader and recorder of the group's observations rather than as the "expert." The theory is that the lessons are learned more deeply and are more likely to be integrated into the students' behavior.

Wanting to catch up with my younger faculty, I adopted this approach in some of my classes. It went OK, but I was quite frustrated. Teaching seemed so inefficient. It took the students eighty minutes to "learn" what I could have stated in ten minutes. The question, however was, would they retain my "lesson" as effectively as they would learning it through an experiential exercise?

This flight from lecturing may have another purpose. Today's faculty are more uncertain of what should be taught. Particularly in management, yesterday's classical "principles" are recognized as conditional. They are not universals. So scholars are very careful to surround their assertions with recognition of their "probabilistic" and "situational" natures. This is valid, but it can be too academic and just plain boring. Students have more fun playing games.

Maturity Missing in Action

I had planned a special class for the final week of the semester. Student teams were to make oral reports electing a new president of a firm based on transcripts of a consultant's interview with the final four candidates. Three teams out of the six in the class were to be picked out of a Bud Lite baseball cap. Plus I had told my students that a guest commentator for the class would be a newly elected CEO of a major firm. He would be able to offer his relevant insights into their recommendations. I was really looking forward to the class.

Three sixty-student sections were to meet 9–10:30 am, 10:30–12:00, and 1:30–3:00 pm. Clearly it was to be a major time commitment by our visiting President. At the appointed time for the first class, only eighteen students were present. Each team's speaker was there so the presentations were made. I didn't want our guest to feel that he had been slighted so I said nothing about the empty seats. And the conversation went well. But of course I was very angry about the poor attendance.

The second course section started with approximately thirty students there – about half the class. The final class ran with almost forty students – still well below average. At the end of the day, I thanked my guest who seemed to have enjoyed the interaction with the students.

That afternoon I spoke to several students to find out why attendance had been so poor. Clearly the teams had been well prepared, but so many members had apparently taken the day off. However, they hadn't slept in or gone golfing. Rather, an accounting exam was scheduled for that evening and most had attended a review session all morning. They had decided that the imminence of the exam dominated the importance of attending a management class. The near term quantifiable task dominated a longer-term qualitative activity. Worse, thy simply didn't even consider the impoliteness of their behavior to me and to our class guest.

I can't judge whether this decision was wrong for students who were having difficulty with accounting. Sometimes one has to focus on an immediate weakness rather than development for the future. Nonetheless, if this is a person's habitual behavior it will lead to continual tyranny of the short run and long run disaster. Repeated short-run thinking is simply immature. The behavior seemed to validate a hypothesis that several other faculty shared with me: that our twenty-eight year old MBA students were seven years behind our 1950's generation in maturity. They behaved as we did at twenty-one.

I certainly lectured my students about this at our next and last class meeting, for which I was criticized on their anonymous teacher evaluation.

NEVER criticize your students at the last class!

Hip Hop Arrives at Wharton

Kevin was an exceptionally well-dressed and handsome Morehouse College graduate. Like many of that fine Atlanta institution's alumni, he possessed remarkable self-confidence and presence. He was a student in my elective course on executive self-management that considers time and career management among other topics. Kevin asked me if I was familiar with a rap group named Kriss Kross. To this staid professor, hip-hop was an unexplored world so I said no. It seems Kevin had been one of the discoverers of two Atlanta twelve year olds then emerging as solid hits in the music world. I subsequently saw a tape of the twosome who, if nothing else, were endowed with phenomenal energy.

Kevin's "problem" was that he was already earning hundreds of thousand of dollars from the group's recordings, but the time demands on him were seriously interfering with his MBA studies. He wanted to quit or postpone program completion, but his mother was adamant that he earn his MBA first. I guess he wanted me to bless his leaving which in general I did – perhaps guided by Omar Khayyam's advice to, "take the cash and let the credit go, nor heed the rumble of a distant drum." I was sure that hip-hop was a flash in the pan, soon to disappear from the entertainment scene. Therefore, Kevin should take a year off, collect the money, and return when the fad had passed. He didn't, and it hasn't.

According to the internet rumor mill, he is involved with Janet Jackson. Not bad for someone who took my faulty advice.

Maureen's Lament

Maureen Daly was the manager of data processing in a medium sized company. I met her when I spoke to a meeting organized by IBM to help management information system managers in client firms. She supervised a department of twelve programmers and operators. At the development session, we discussed managerial leadership. I had emphasized that sometimes a manager must simply make a decision with little consultation, especially on minor matters or even major issues in a crisis situation when time is of the essence.

After the meeting, Maureen said to me: "I enjoyed your talk, but I didn't like your bias in favor of autocratic management. It seems old-fashioned and insensitive."

I replied that I didn't mean to be biased, but that I used the term "authoritarian," not "autocratic."

Maureen continued, "Well maybe, but I think most young managers today know that they just can't make decisions unilaterally and order subordinates around. People don't like to be dictated to; they want to feel that they are involved. They need to participate in departmental decisions."

I asked if that was the way she ran her department.

"Yes. Every morning I have a meeting with my staff to discuss what has to be done that day and what problems exist. We strive to reach consensus on each issue before going on."

My reply to Maureen was that it sounds good so what was her problem.

Maureen said, "Two weeks ago I had my annual merit review and am still distressed about what the vice president told me. He said I didn't have control of my department; that things were drifting; that two of my senior staff had gone to him complaining about the time wasted in meetings deciding 'where to locate the coffee machine.' They complained that I had difficulty making decisions. The VP also told me that there have been reports of horseplay on the night shift involving a water pistol fight I never heard about. He said that unless things changed my promotion potential was limited. I try to treat my people as adults, respect their opinions, invite their participation, and motivate them to set their own performance standards. But they seem to behave like children, some of them anyway. And my senior staff go around my back to complain."

Maureen concluded. "Perhaps you're right."

I asked "About what?"

"That managers should be autocrats."

"But that's not what I said!"

Jackie Robinson and the Best and Worse Days

It was a glorious day on a golf course in the May Charleston sun. One newly retired foursome member in delight exclaimed: "Ah, the worst day on the golf course is better than the best day at work." I could only think what a lousy career he must have had. How different from the wonderful days that I experienced.

Nonetheless, his observation on worst and best leads me to think about my peak and valley school experiences. During my years as head of Penn's fundraising there were plenty of candidates for the worst: when two Penn alumni committed $25,000,000 to two Texas institutions, UT Austin and SMU (Texas was the most difficult state to get money out of because Penn alumni living there are so loyal to their home). Or worst, when Coca Cola's Robert Woodruff gave $100,000,000,000 to Emory just a month after I had turned down a job offer there.

Upon reflection, however, both the best and worst days involved the same person, Jack Roosevelt Robinson – Jackie Robinson of Brooklyn Dodger fame. I was traveling on university business when in an airport I saw a familiar white haired head accompanied by a strikingly attractive woman. It was Jack and his wife Rachel. I had never met either, but from a lifetime of admiration felt that I had. Departing totally from my practice of not bugging celebrities in public, I introduced myself and told him what his success in Brooklyn had meant to a suburban New York boy. He replied graciously in that squeaking high voice. It was thrilling.

Unhappily, Jack was already seriously ill and not long afterward he died.. I learned of it just before teaching an undergraduate class in organizational behavior. My twenty-year-olds must have wondered why I had tears in my eyes as I explained what Jack had meant to my friends and me. In my neighborhood, to express opposition to the "establishment," one rooted for the Dodgers rather than the New York Yankees. It reflected our youthful support for underdogs. And Jack arrived in 1947 as the ultimate underdog. In our idealism and naiveté, his sterling character, seemingly inexhaustible patience, and athletic brilliance would end racial prejudice. Even more, we thought that his example would unlock the potential energy for achievement among black Americans. And Black America would be the new driving force for American greatness.

But of course, we were only 13 years old. The Yankees continued to win the World Series and problems for America and its black citizens persisted. At age 46, I cried in class for Jack of course, but also for the loss of innocence and idealism that his passing represented. I cried for me.

But maybe that authentic expression made a more lasting impression on my students than that day's assignment on expectancy theory.

Teaching Students Who Are Just Too Good

The most unsatisfying teaching I ever did was a one evening a week religion class for high school seniors. I taught these wonderful young people for five years. I have no sense that I had any impact at all.

Why? The kids were marvelous, but in general, they were the children of parents who forced them to continue religion class through high school when most of their friends had long since bugged out of attending. They basically did what their parents told them to do.

The problem was that they accepted everything on faith. I couldn't generate much discussion. No conflicting ideas were expressed. In time, I resorted to trying to generate conflict by posing non-traditional (probably heretical) questions. Why were many people attracted to atheism? Why did religion appear to create so much hatred? Suppose men had created God in his (her?) own image, rather the scriptural verse's opposite? I even threw in some of Karl Marx's views. It was during the Vietnam War and I expressed my horror at New York's Cardinal Spellman's statement that God was on America's side.

I image some parents were horrified to hear what we were discussing in religion class (if their children even told them). But I never received any complaints, not even from the parish rector. Attending religion class seemed to be more ritualistic than substantial.

Good teaching demands some student resistance. Differences of opinion need to be expressed in order for learning to occur. I felt my high school religion class students were just too good to be true. But, was I just too cynical?

Coaching the Johnson School Quarterpounders

No one beats a daughter in eliciting feelings of guilt. Back in the early 1970's, I, like most of my contemporaries who attended all male colleges, was surprised by how angry so many women were. As a ten year old, she helped me to understand.

My daughter asked me to coach their school recreation league softball team. This was a volunteer activity that I had always avoided for her older brother. I would rationalize that I was just too busy at the university to coach Little League baseball or Pop Warner football. And I knew nothing about soccer. My daughter, however, cleverly played to my guilt by saying that plenty of fathers offered to coach the boys, but no one wanted to coach the girls.

I did know something about baseball having played for years. Jennifer and I (and her mother) frequently played catch together. I had read that Mickey Mantle's father had stood him in front of their barn and thrown a ball to him as hard as he could. I didn't have the barn, but I had emulated Mickey's Dad and ten-year-old Jennifer's return throws were already stinging my hand.

So I accepted her call. It came to be one of the greatest experiences of my life. Much of what I learned about feminism and female aspirations grew out of coaching the Johnson School Quarterpounders (named, of course, after their favorite food, the now politically incorrect MacDonald's big burger).

I believed it was important to the girls that I be serious in my coaching and that my expectations be high. Jennifer and I had already been subjects in a Temple University Psychology student's research comparing father interactions with sons and daughters. Supposedly, I was part of a minority twenty percent that communicated similar performance expectations to both son and daughter (most fathers expected and encouraged higher performance from their sons). I tried to apply this to my coaching.

Most important was to teach the girls to respect but not be afraid of the ball. Early practice consisted of standing in a circle throwing the ball randomly (and deceptively). Muffs were perfectly acceptable. Indeed, I wanted them to experience some pain from missed balls. The key lesson was that one must carry on for the team even when hurting and tears cloud your vision. Practice would end with me racing all the girls who seemed to try much harder to beat me than each other. In time, most did.

The Quarterpounders became a very successful team. Beating our opponents was fun, but the great thrill was watching the girls discover what they were capable of. Even more satisfying was seeing them repeatedly increase their self-expectations. The growth in confidence from ten to twelve was stupendous. Twelve-year-old girls can do anything – or so it seemed to me.

Back in the 1950's Margaret Mead argued that young girls were handicapped by the lack of experience on competitive teams. Whereas boys generally made-up teams based on known performance, girls chose teammates based mainly on friendships. Therefore, they just didn't experience the linkage between results and building a team based on objective performance data. More fundamentally, in Mead's thesis, girls missed out on the agony of defeat and the thrill of victory (to use ABC's old Olympic cliché). The Quarterpounders experienced more of the up side than the down, but both were valuable.

I don't know the subsequent histories of all the players, but my daughter batted over .500 for her junior high school team before shifting to lacrosse where she became first team all-Ivy at Penn. Our second basemen showed up years later in my graduate course in management. After graduating from William and Mary, the first baseman earned her doctorate from Penn in educational psychology.

Perhaps I was a better softball coach than university professor.

II. Managing

What if my Staff Reads My Books?

I never really understood the meaning of the phrase, "hoist on his own petard" until I was. I taught managerial psychology with a particular interest in career development, life transitions, and, of course, the clichéd "mid-life crisis." I had been quite creative in recommending courageous strategies to remain vital by confronting change and embracing the ambiguous. The words of Soren Kierkegaard dropped easily in my talks with students and executives: "To venture is to face anxiety, but not to venture is to lose oneself."

All of this made me fair game for a persuasive president who urged me to put my behavior where my words were: to leave a comfortable and prestigious professorship for the challenges of leading a department of over 100 people engaged in alumni relations, public relations and fundraising.

My first concern was that I couldn't possibly be as effective a manager as my textbooks suggested I should. Since I had written management textbooks and articles about effective leadership and human resource management, my theoretical views were all too available perhaps leading to elevated expectations of my managerial skills. The gap between theory and practice is real to every management teacher, but it looms particularly threatening once one is trying to jump over it. Between theory and practice falls the shadow. Management books are so rational; they imply that executives are always conscious of what they're doing and why. But they aren't. The emotional component is much greater than expected.

Accordingly, at my first meeting with my new staff, I told them they should feel free to purchase any of my books, BUT UNDER NO CIRCUMSTANCES SHOULD THEY READ THEM!

The Dog Ate My Budget

I would often ask my students to fill in the blank in the following sentence: "_____ is the only thing that I do that when I'm doing it I don't think I should be doing something else." Usually after some laughter, I would state that "SEX" may be a truthful answer, but look for another activity. The question was once poised by Gloria Steinem in explaining her choice of journalism as a career. Her answer (and mine) was "writing."

I've written ten books, a hundred articles and thousands of letters and memoranda, all, I hope, benefiting from the trauma of a "D" I had received in my first writing assignment in college freshman English. I was devastated. After all, I had been a "star" at New Rochelle High School! It was critique of John Keats's poem *Lamia* written with all the pretentiousness that I thought Princeton expected. It took me some time to understand the lesson of that long forgotten grader: to write simply with definitive sentences (obviously he was a devotee of Strunk and White's, *ELEMENTS OF STYLE*). My dubious success was only evident many years later in my academic career at Penn when a colleague observed about one of my books that I would never be promoted to full professor because my writing was "too easy to understand." I now recognize that this simplicity was due less to my clear writing than to my inability to think more complex thoughts.

Still I was eventually promoted to professor, which according to rumors, was because I was seen as having "administrative potential." In other words, I was fated to be one of those academics who accepted "promotions" into such dreaded administrative posts as "Assistant to," "Department Chair," and "Vice President." Once I reached these elevated positions, I quickly learned the critical managerial skill of writing budgets, reports and memoranda that no one could understand. This was fine, except that even I sometimes couldn't decipher what I had meant.

My skill at administrative obfuscation peaked, however, quite by accident. When still a new VP, I had spread out all of the departmental budget requests on my dining room table so I could take a couple of days circling the table and contemplating priorities. At some point, an errant breeze blew some sheets onto the floor where they were chewed up by my Golden Retriever Rebecca. Later when I announced the new budget to my assembled troops, it was pointed out that a $100,000 request was missing. It quite embarrassing to give the excuse: "the dog ate my budget" – a claim not unlike those voiced by my former students about late reports.

My accounting acumen led to my serving on the boards of directors and audit committees of two large international corporations and a university medical center. All had annual budgets in the millions so my missing $100,000 would not even have been noticed. I was even elected Vice Chairman of one of these organizations, which proves that simple mindedness pays off, in the business world if not in academe.

Gainful Pain

Being rejected for promotion is a pain anywhere at any time. But in academia it can be a special threat because most schools operate on an "up or out" basis. A young Lecturer or Assistant Professor must earn promotion to tenured Associate Professor within a limited time-period, generally six years. As a department head, I had to counsel many rejected young scholars of promise who felt that there was no valid life outside the Ivy League. If pain leads to gain, as the athletic cliché puts it, then I was a beneficiary.

On leaving graduate school, I was hired as a lecturer by the management department chairman at the Wharton School. H was an extremely strong leader who pushed hard for productivity while also acting as benevolent father. He assigned me to be a teaching assistant in his industrial relations course where he valued my ability to teach a class on short notice if he was unable to make it because of his active outside affairs. He was very helpful in personal matters, inviting me to share in his consulting and getting a prestigious university physician to travel out of state to treat my seriously ill son. In two years, he saw that I was promoted to Assistant Professor.

Five years later, however, to the surprise of both my mentor and me my promotion to tenured associate professor was rejected by our department faculty. The department head announced his resignation because, in his view, his senior colleagues had blocked my promotion in retaliation for their disagreement with him about department policy. More likely, it was his authoritarian leadership style.

My vulnerability as a protégé to a disliked department head was evident in my being rejected. I was in effect a political pawn. Of course it was not "fair" because I was judged by my association rather than the merits of my work. There was nothing I could do to change the past, but I could work on the future.

I approached the full professor who seemed most opposed to the former department head to open a dialogue, not about the unfairness of my rejection, but around shared interests. I asked for copies of his papers, sent him copies of mine, and sought his suggestions. I tried to sit at the same luncheon table with him at least once a week. It all sounds quite manipulative in the retelling, but I discovered that our interests and values were actually more similar than they had ever been with my former mentor. I came to admire this senior colleague very much. The appointment of a new department head and the now active support of my new sponsor led to my promotion sailing through after a transition year.

However self-seeking my intentions in reaching out to the senior colleague who became my second mentor, it led to a long-lasting relationship greatly valued by us both. After his death, his widow told me that when he went into the hospital for his final losing battle with leukemia, he took with him a note that I had sent him expressing my gratitude for what he had taught me about academic life and human values. I still miss him

I was lucky in that my initial promotion rejection forced me to be more assertive in reaching out to other older colleagues. Pain did produce gain.

An Abortıve Faculty Revolt

I am embarrassed to admit that I once participated in an attempted departmental *coup d'e-tat*. Management research and teaching was shifting its basic underlying disciplines from labor economics and political theory to psychology and social psychology. Faculty trained in the emerging disciplines were mainly non-tenured juniors who felt that their career progress was being impeded by the dominance of the older orientation.

Knowing that their political clout was too little to effect change, they asked me to become an ally. Although I agreed with their goals, as an Associate Professor I recognized that we needed a more prestigious leader. There was an older professor of international renown in our field who had just joined the faculty. We appealed to him. He agreed to serve as titular head of a new "unit" if I would do the administrative chores.

Emboldened, we approached the Management Department Head to negotiate either full or partial independence. This was a mistake, however, for he was a wily politician. He responded with an invitation to take all of us out to dinner. After several rounds of drinks, our secession evaporated when our nominal leader, who suffered from narcolepsy, fell asleep at the table. The revolt never awakened.

Years later when I became Chairman, I thought how fortunate that my predecessor had forestalled the threatened faculty split. Cut loose from the power of being in the school's largest department, our little cabal would have had little clout to hire faculty and get them promoted. As a former Department Head repeatedly advised me, "Ross, never, **never, NEVER** voluntarily give up any power!"

"I'm Going to Try to Get Pregnant Tonight"

These words were conveyed to me by a young woman Assistant Professor. As a newly appointed Department Chair, I had been surprised by the degree of intimate involvement a Chairman had in his faculty's lives, but this set a new high for intimacy.

My young colleague was not seeking permission. She was, after all, married. Rather, she wanted to convey that she had planned the birth to occur during the summer before her non-teaching semester so that her newborn's demands would not interfere with her ability to retain her full time research and teaching load. To adhere to her detailed schedule, however, she and her husband had a small window in which to conceive their child. That night was to mark the window's opening. I can only hope that her husband was aware of the schedule she had planned for him. As *Sex in the City*'s Samantha Jones once observed after a one-night fling playing the male role in a lesbian relationship, "I never knew that men had to work so hard!"

Of course, in academe it is women who especially have to work hard if they are too meet research and publication expectations as well as maintain a relationship with a loved one and eventually become a parent. Earning tenure at a major research university generally requires a six to nine year trial period after earning one's doctorate. The biological clock begins to tick louder as one passes thirty-five or so. Under pressure from woman colleagues, institutions have struggled to define equitable policies that recognize the challenges.

As a father of five, I tried to persuade my intimate informer that she might want to consider taking a year's leave (no salary, but continuation of paid benefits) with the guarantee that she would be given an additional year before the tenure clock expired. She was reluctant to accept this option because she was skeptical that her male colleagues wouldn't resent her extra year. After all, young male faculty upon fatherhood never exercised this option. Plus, she felt she could do it all and retain full salary. Ah, the optimism of youth!

But she did and eleven months later she demonstrated how well she combined career and motherhood (and showed me the breast pump that she kept in her office – which operation, thankfully, she didn't offer to demonstrate).

Firing a Prized Recruit

Recruiting a highly prized new Assistant Professor and seeing him or her fail to become productive in research and teaching is a disappointment. But having to fire a promising young scholar because of improper sex with a student is infuriating. It certainly made me angry.

The best newly minted Ph.D.'s in behavioral economics and decision theory are in great demand. Recruiting them is time consuming and expensive. A Department Head usually makes a significant personal investment in developing a relationship with the candidate. Often the courting process involves negotiation about an eclectic mix of desires. One candidate requested that I pay for in-vitro fertilization (at a cost of $10,000 per try) because he and his wife were having difficulty becoming pregnant. And I did.

From the beginning, Professor X behaved a bit like an immature spoiled brat. He missed a commitment to finish his doctoral dissertation; he criticized older senior faculty in public for being "obsolete." Nonetheless, his potential was impressive – until I received a call that an undergraduate nursing student had charged that he had raped her. Apparently they had met in an off campus bar. He said that she was twenty-two years old, was not a student in his school, would never be in one of his classes, and that the sex had been consensual. It quickly became a "she said," "he said" affair. To make the situation murkier, the accuser later declined to press charges so the matter was dropped by the police.

University rules clearly proscribed sex between a professor and a student currently in or possibly in the future one of his/her classes. Rules now prohibit sex between any professor and undergraduate students. And "moral turpitude" is grounds for dismissal.

For me, Professor X's behavior was a most profound violation of the moral obligations of the implicit authority relationship between a faculty member and a student. I wanted him out.

But abrogating an employment contract is not easy. Since there were no legal charges, getting him to depart became a negotiation rather than an exercise in authority. It ended up costing my school a large, but undisclosed amount of money. I, in effect, funded a lengthy vacation.

As time passed, I have wondered if I was too zealous in curtailing this young professor's career at Penn. Perhaps I was so angry because I had invested so much in recruiting him; or because his behavior was so contrary to my personal morals. Did I blame him as an ungrateful son? Did I place my own interests ahead of the university's?

Be Careful if you Practice
What You Teach

When I was a Columbia graduate student, two full professors left Morningside Heights and defected to the allures of Palo Alto and Stanford University. The gossip on campus in New York was that they were the first two full professors ever to leave for another university in the almost two hundred-year history of the former Kings College. How the academic world has changed since then.

During most of the booming economy of the last twenty years, retention has been even more important than recruiting. So much is invested in recruiting an employee, perhaps especially young assistant professors, that retaining the best requires constant attention. To get a better sense of what this required, I would attend human-resource-manager business conventions where the theme was focusing on the best. That is, during annual performance evaluation and compensation decisions, managers should ask who are the most important ten percent of personnel most critical to the future of my organizational unit? These are the people to invest in.

My university, like most others, annually issued quite strict salary increase guidelines. Typically, this took the form of defining a 3 percent total salary increase pool with the recommended range being from 1 to 6 percent. Any salary change between 6 and 9 percent required a special letter (as did anything less than 1 percent). A recommendation for an increase over 10 percent required, in effect, permission in advance from the Dean. The intent clearly was to force administrators to narrow their differentiation among staff.

At a private institution, salaries are supposedly confidential, but leaks and rumors are rampant. So even though the actually monetary differences are quite small, they can loom large symbolically. Most department heads try to avoid controversy by giving almost everyone the three percent raise. For retention objectives, however, this is precisely the wrong approach.

The dominant theme in today's compensation is greater differentiation between outstanding performers and the rest. It is the exceptionally valuable ones that one strives to retain. As a new department head, I followed this advice. Analyzing whom I thought the most important faculty for the department's future was relatively easy. The present and future stars were five (out of a total count of 40 standing faculty) tenured Associate Professors, most two or more years away from full professorships. I went to bat for ten percent plus salary increases for them. But this of course put severe pressure on my total salary pool. I got a few extra bucks from the Dean, but not enough to allow anything greater than three percent or less salary increases for the rest of the faculty. Indeed, I went to two percent for some of the less productive just to shave a few dollars off the total.

How proud I was of my self to make such a courageous decision! I withstood my colleagues' complaints. But then I was threatened with a suit for age discrimination. An older full professor with whom I had discussed my compensation philosophy said I had discriminated against faculty nearer the end of their careers. Of course, he was correct. I had not included any full professors in my list of most-important-to-the-future category.

The suit never succeeded, but the experience reinforced that life is easier when an administrator just gives everyone the same pool mandated salary increase. If a star receives a competitive offer, you can then kick the issue upstairs to the Dean or Provost saying that if they want to retain the young Einstein they had better produce the necessary moola.

Unhappily, once he or she has sampled the delights of California, it is tough to lure either back to Philadelphia. Better to keep them so happy that they don't make the trip.

A Departmental *Ménage a Quatre*

What is it about women when they divorce? Almost overnight, they lose weight, put on makeup, and appear transformed – or so it seems to this aging male. I've read the articles on how newly unmarried women suffer income decline and ostracism by friends. Nonetheless, the new independence can be a powerful self-growth motivator.

So the metamorphosis unfolded in our academic department. A recently divorced associate professor became transformed into an object of intense attraction to three of her married colleagues. The cocoon to butterfly transformation in this case is no unrealistic poetic metaphor. As a young teacher, her attire had been denim grunge. Devoid of any accessories to draw attention away from the patchy jeans, her appearance was even worse than her students'. And they just didn't take her seriously.

Out of concern for her professional future, our female Dean eventually called her into her office for a talk about appropriate academic attire. This led to some improvement but nothing like the post divorce change.

Is all this attention to clothing and appearance relevant to evaluating our colleague's scholarly work? Of course not. And it didn't have any impact. She was generally seen as a research and writing star publishing in the best journals in her field.

Socially, however, her stock rose. Do silly men just look differently upon a divorced woman? Perhaps each deludes himself that she wasn't satisfied by the former partner and so "I" am the one to satisfy her? More modestly, perhaps each thinks she is an easy mark who would be grateful for any attention.

Whatever. But three of her colleagues became infatuated with our newly freed star. They wanted to sit on committees with her, to jointly write papers, co-teach courses, and attend distant conferences with her. From previously eating from the trucks alone at her desk, her admirers individually invited her out to lunch.

It was comical to observe even if a bit disturbing because I knew all their wives. Perhaps they were just being kindly to someone they thought needed a friend. I didn't feel it was my place as the department head to warn anyone. But then one of the threesome came to me complaining that the romantic competition was undermining the relationship of at least two of them who had to work together on a common course.

In time, the situation resolved itself. The would-be paramour who apparently felt the most guilt decided to follow his wife to another school from which she had received an offer. And in time, it seemed that one of her attentive followers had indeed been motivated mainly by concern rather than lust. They evolved into friends. Unhappily, she ended the relationship with the third suitor by resigning and moving to another university a long distance away.

I hated to see her go. Could I have prevented it? Doubtful. Some personnel problems are beyond a department head's power. The episode, however, did certainly reinforce my happiness with my own happy marriage!

Why Woman Faculty are Smarter than Men

I tread carefully here. An esteemed scholar much my superior lost his Harvard presidency, in part because of his awkward expressing of a theory about women's supposed lack of aptitude for academic science. So let me explain the basis of my assertion.

When I began recruiting faculty thirty years ago, the Wharton School would generally get whomever they made an offer to (with the possible exception of two competitors whom I shall judiciously omit identifying to protect our status). In those days virtually all my offers were to males.

As the years passed our success rate fell a bit, but this was easily explained by the ferocious competition for minority and female candidates. But I began to notice that we were losing highly desired new faculty to schools, which, in our unbiased opinion, were of lower eminence. We could no longer assume that our reputation would carry the day.

Even worse, some of the women who accepted our offers and were appointed Assistant Professors, and compiled attractive records, left before being considered for tenure. No such pattern characterized young male faculty. What was going on? When I spoke to the young women who rejected us (yes, I admit it felt a little like they were rejecting ME), I would hear varied reasons: "My parents are old and ill and I don't want to be so far away;" – "My husband has a good job in New York City and we need to live closer;" – "I would prefer to be at a teaching institution where there is less pressure for research."

In no way am I trivializing these decision criteria. Women scholars tend to have a more complex decision matrix than most men. Most of our male candidates focused on how their professional careers would be served. Modern women, however, are trying to balance a larger and more complex set of criteria. They are trying to satisfy on multiple dimensions rather than optimizing one. In short, they are more motivated to balance their lives around their various roles as researcher, teacher, wife, daughter, mother, and human being. For this they are certainly wiser than most male faculty.

I well remember one colleague who resigned when ready for promotion to full professor by saying that she, "just don't want to do the administrative chores that Ross does for the rest of my life." Now, that was wisdom!

Margaret Offends the Faculty Feminists

Some years after she retired as the United Kingdom Prime Minister, Lady Margaret Thatcher was invited by the Dean of the Annenberg School for Communication to talk about the role of the media in politics. Invitations were extended to all university faculty and scheduled for the largest campus auditorium. The audience included most of the faculty movers and shakers so naturally it had a significantly liberal tone.

Bouffant hairdo firmly lacquered in place, Lady Thatcher strode to the podium and declared that she was going to tear up her speech, which she did. Perhaps motivated by unfolding events in the Balkans and the Middle East, she announced that she would talk instead about what we owed to dead white English males. And so she did, off the cuff, and brilliantly.

Restlessness, however, began to percolate throughout the auditorium. This is not what the faculty liberals had come to hear. Thatcher was drilling home the contributions of due process, habeas corpus, parliamentary government, and the free market which she argued were so strikingly absent from most of the nations on the UN's Human Rights Committee. As bad as the British Empire was reputed to have been, she argued that her former colonies demonstrated strikingly freer and more vibrant political life that any Muslim country, etc., etc. Here and there, individuals began to depart for suddenly remembered more pressing engagements.

Margaret Thatcher has generally been more attractive to men than to women. During the years she was in office, I would conduct a survey in various classes asking: "Name a contemporary person (alive or deceased, but overlapping your lifetime) who, for you, best represents the concept of 'leader.'" Among mid-career Wharton Executive Program participants, out of thirty votes Thatcher generally would receive three to four, the most of any woman. But all from males; **no** female executive ever named Thatcher. The women so cited by women (Mother Teresa) were generally seen as being involved in more humane activity. Perhaps Thatcher was seen as too cold, too male-like, or too close to Ronald Reagan.

By the end of her address, the audience was somewhat older, whiter, maler and more conservative.

Why Did The Deans Boo Me?

As a professor, I once had the rare opportunity to address a room full of Deans and other senior administrators (thankfully, at another university, not my own). We were talking about managerial incentives so I described a business executive famous for his motivational skills – Jack Welch then General Electric's CEO. Jack was a fierce budget negotiator who created a high reward-risk culture for making one's budget. This didn't bother my audience.

What provoked their outburst was my description of Welch's creation of a kind of "play money" which was allocated to successful managers to facilitate experimentation. That is, a department head might be given a million bucks without strings attached. He or she couldn't use the funds to buy a yacht or gamble in Las Vegas, but to encourage change in a department's products or processes. Success might bring accolades and more discretionary funds in the next budget, but less shiny results incurred no punishment. It was at this point that my august academic listeners shifted to angry baseball fan boos.

I was taken aback. Did they think that Welch was profligate? Did they dislike the idea that people at work might actually be innovative? Or have fun? No. What bugged them was envy. University budgets are notorious for inflexibility. No slack exists. Opportunities that arise in the course of the budget year usually just have to wait until after the next budget is negotiated Given that the budget cycle at their state institution could take two years, by then the opportunity might be gone or forgotten. They simply wished that they could have more discretionary funds.

A few years later, when I became Penn's Vice President, I pushed our Executive Budget Director on this issue, pointing out that the Development Department at Yale could keep some portion of the money raised beyond their target to play with, that Princeton seemed to have some kind of a "secret" discretionary budget outside of the faculty's prying eyes, and that Brown seem to be so marvelously flexible and playful in their public communications.

I didn't get booed, but I didn't convince him either.

Of Cocktails and Presidents

Reginald Jones, former Chairman of General Electric once observed that he frequently invited senior GE executives and their spouses to Board of Directors' parties because it was important to observe how they "handled alcohol." Attending MANY cocktail parties has always characterized the managerial positions that I've held. I tried to prep myself in advance on the names of the expected attendees. But a drink or two can fog one's memory and twist one's tongue. I once greeted a large donor's first "starter" wife with the name of his second "trophy" wife. She was not pleased.

In addition to learning how to handle alcohol myself, at receptions for various university presidents, I've had an opportunity to observe their drinking and how they were handling stress. A clear stress indicator is an executive's inability to focus on the person with whom he or she is talking. Those feeling harassed are always looking around in fear of what alumnus may be the next complainant or professor a petitioner for a bigger budget. It is often painfully obvious that the President is not enjoying the talk and frantically looking for an escape route. Often an aid is prepped to give a phony excuse for an early departure.

After Ray Smith became CEO of Bell Atlantic, he initiated a management development program that emphasized "be here now" as its theme. His point was that managers need to control their own anxieties and focus on the immediate conversation if they were to truly LISTEN. At the JFK Library in Boston, a common theme on the oral history tapes is Kennedy's ability to focus. When you got to see him, he listened as if you were the most important person on his calendar.

The best university practitioner in my experience was former Yale President (and baseball commissioner) Bart Giamatti. We were once sitting together at a dinner of numberless speeches. I asked him how he handled so seemingly effortlessly the endless complaints that came his way. He responded that to him "Life was simply too short and I have too many interesting things I want to do to worry about naysayers." His equanimity might have been helped by the cigarette smoking he was sneaking in this non-smoking venue by hiding underneath the table.

Alas, Bart's life turned out to be too short for what he wanted to do. He died at age fifty-one of a massive heart attack.

Drinking on Campus

As young Lieutenant in the United States Navy, I was once assigned as a liaison with the Royal Canadian Navy serving on a Halifax based Corvette. What struck me first about the ship was how much more attractive their sea foam green paint was to our battleship gray (I have no idea, however, which provided better camouflage). The second impression was the different rules regarding alcoholic beverages in the Officer's Mess. The American Navy simply forbids all alcohol on board ship. The Canadians allow an open bar.

When I conveyed this information to my U.S. Navy junior colleagues the consensus was that however attractive such a policy, it would not work with Americans. We would all imbibe excessively – as we certainly did when off the ship on shore leave. But with rare exceptions, the Canadian officers did not drink to excess, especially on board ship. The social norms were not explicit, but they were clear. It was simply unacceptable to allow alcohol to affect your ability to stand duty. And it was not done.

Years later as father of a college student son the whole issue of social or personal alcohol control arose again. The drinking age in the United States is twenty–one, but binge drinking has become a major problem on our college campuses. One student said to me, "If they are going to treat us like children, we will behave like children." So the alcohol is purchased illegally and consumed to excess in fraternities, dorm rooms, and private homes. It is so different in the best college town I've ever seen – Saint Andrews in Scotland. There the student dorms surround the town center which is chock full of restaurants and bars. The drinking age is eighteen and students simply walk a few hundred feet to town to drink in public along with the town's other residents. The whole scene is more adult and civilized than in the U.S. where we segregate college students from real life.

Town and gown should be more integrated and the legal drinking age should be eighteen. Have student live as the adults they claim to be.

Disappearing Martinis

How ironic that as student binge drinking was increasing, faculty drinking was disappearing – at least at lunch. When I started teaching, groups of the then virtually all-male professors would dine together at The Faculty Club. As you entered the hall, the first buffet station was a complete bar manned by a beloved attendant who knew most of the older men's standards. One or two martini's before lunch was not at all uncommon among the senior august personages with whom I had the honor to dine. Today the bar and drinks are gone with the wind, along with the culture that sustained them. What went wrong? Or right?

So many things changed in the academy. Foremost in changing luncheon patterns were increased competition, student class preferences, and the expansion of female colleagues. Like other areas of American life, the competition for tenure and status sharply increased leading to enhanced pressure for faculty to obtain research grants and publish. One couldn't afford the quiet post-drink nap back in the office.

Even more striking, one seldom had the afternoon totally free of classes. Students began demanding that courses, especially electives, be scheduled no earlier that 9:00 or 10:00 am. Gone were the 7:40's of my college days. This meant that to attract enrollment a professor had to schedule more classes in the afternoon. And to keep students awake and the course attractive to future enrollees, he had to personally stay awake – all but impossible after a noonday martini.

Finally, younger faculty were less interested in the faculty club ritual. Woman especially preferred to buy their sandwich wraps from the ubiquitous campus trucks and retreat to their offices eating alone and capturing time to work. Compared to the former 60-75 minutes, we are now down to about ten minutes for lunch.

Time and productivity have been gained, but social life has suffered. The grapevine has fewer fruit. Women faculty complain about being isolated and not engaged. Informal policy debates now require the dreaded formally scheduled meetings.

For years I disliked the trucks, but now in retirement I rather enjoy sitting outside alone without an afternoon agenda just soaking in the campus energy.

Missing Secretaries

Forty years ago an ambition of every newly minted Assistant Professor was to escape from having to share a secretary with two or three colleagues. Today, the ratio is more like one to eight to ten professors. The personal computer has eliminated secretaries – and those remaining transformed into administrative assistants. Now, Ph.D.'s do their own typing.

And they like it. Gone is the awkwardness of a male professional handing indecipherable handwriting to be typed by a twenty year old typist – as well as the even greater awkwardness of a thirty year old woman professor giving work to the typists, We don't know how the missing typists feel, but the faculty like the control of their writing and communicating that the computer allows. No more delay because your handwriting was so bad that your manuscript was slid to the bottom of the "to be typed" pile. No more bickering with the secretarial pool by snobbish professors who felt that their elevated status justified priority treatment (well, less of it anyway).

In general, the departmental climate is quieter because interdependence between faculty and staff has been reduced. They need to talk less. And the PC for this and other reasons has contributed mightily to a dramatic increase in faculty research, articles, and books. But something has been lost as desks in the open areas disappeared and more work was done behind closed faculty office doors.

Seductive Office Furnishings

Office space and furniture can be seductive, especially to a newly promoted administrator. I was once a director of a corporation whose new CEO had taken as his office a significant share of a newly constructed addition to the headquarters building. Inviting the board chairman and me to view his proud creation, which he had designed and decorated himself, was a harbinger of the faults that subsequently led to his forced departure. The space was just so over the top. Oriental rugs, mahogany cabinets, leather couches and grandfather clock all screamed of an ego out of control. The expense itself was less of a concern than the power isolation that his space communicated. Here was a person not likely to listen to his subordinates. Indeed, the carpeting itself seemed to warn visitors, "Don't wear your muddy shoes on me!"

Although perhaps having somewhat fewer funds to waste, a newly appointed university Executive Vice President made an equally ill-advised redesign. Insistent that his office be in the same building and hall as the President, he commandeered offices of two middle level administrators to combine into one large space more suited to his self-image. And over $100,000 was spent on the process – quite enormous for academia at the time. But he had come from the business world, so what did he know.

Like our short-termed corporate CEO, this Executive V.P. lasted only a short time. His authoritarian personal style was as ill suited to university life as his office furnishings were incompatible in a world where old desks remain forever, Even worse, the EXP headed all of the non-academic divisions whose personnel were mainly located in a high rise non-academic type building on the campus edge. He actually had only two secretaries in College Hall. To speak to him in person required subordinates to make a substantial walk across campus. There were no spontaneous encounters in the hall. Virtually all meetings would be formally scheduled. His isolation cried out like the CEO carpet, "Don't bother me; I'm too important."

How wise was his successor. Helen O'Bannon had been an Associate Dean at Carnegie Mellon University and Secretary of Welfare in the Commonwealth of Pennsylvania. Seeing her proposed office and hearing of her predecessor's disaster, she sought guidance on where she should locate. Her feminist colleagues were adamant that she must be close to the ultimate power in College Hall. Her centrality would convey a powerful message of the power of the first woman to rise to such a level at Penn. Helen, however, was mainly interested in functionality, not symbols. She recognized the desirability of being close enough for informal conversation with her vice presidents for Finance, Human Resources, and Operational Services. So she chose to move into the Franklin Building, in the office just above mine. It was a wise decision. And besides, it gave both of us an excuse for a nice walk and talk across campus when we had to meet with the President or Provost.

On a university campus, one must be able simultaneously to walk and talk.

The Ghosts of Blockley

For a year during the renovation of its 1950's building, the Wharton School faculty moved to the medical complex into a building named Blockley Hall. It had been abandoned for some time, but its previous occupants had been student nurses enrolled in the hospital nursing school of the Philadelphia General Hospital.

PGH was the public charity hospital for a city with a large number of indigent residents. Old timers referred to PGH affectionately as "Old Blockley." The buildings were certainly nineteenth century old and badly needed renovation. The city government was reluctant to make major investments. Fortunately for the city's budget, the adjacent university medical center and a private children's hospital were in need of more space. So a deal was struck: a consortium of health care institutions took over both PGH's land and mission.

There was no way to effectively use the existing buildings so they were torn down. The demolition repeatedly uncovered ghosts of PGH's past. Out of the wreckage and upturned earth, emerged skeletons and bones attributed to slaves, indigent patients, and anatomy class cadavers. Looking out of my former nursing student's dorm room, I could see the excavation crews and anthropologists discussing their latest finds.

Even with the disappearance of the PGH Nursing School, two others remained on the medical complex: the three year Registered Nurse program in the Hospital of the University of Pennsylvania and the four-year Bachelor of Nursing program in Penn's School of Nursing. The two programs existed in uneasy association, sharing a nursing education building that had been designed to minimize contact between faculty and students in the two programs.

The ideological divide was substantial. The HUP program was dominated by a physician-oriented philosophy that stressed a traditional, somewhat subservient, breed of nurses. Their education emphasized clinical and applied skills. In contrast, the collegiate School of Nursing pushed for more professional and assertive graduates grounded in medical science. In the larger political realm, the B.S.N. advocates were lobbying state legislatures to require a four-year degree in order to be licensed as a registered nurse. Many in the traditional three-year hospital nursing programs saw this as a naked feminist power play.

At the time, I was teaching a management course for the School of Nursing so I understood the logic of their aspirations. But, gazing out of the slowly filling space formally occupied by Old Blockley, I would wonder how the ghosts of the long dead PGH nurses, who worked so faithfully at the bottom rung of American medicine, felt about the debate.

Are Dorms Hotels or Camps?

I was asked to mediate a dispute between the university Department of Operational Services and the Department of Student Life. The conflict centered on maintenance of the student dormitories. Repairs were the responsibility of the university's central department of operational services. Although ultimately the separate chains of command converged at the President, operationally they were separate with Ops Services reporting to the university Executive Vice President (for business services) and Student Life reporting to the Provost who was the chief academic officer.

Students complained about leaking faucets, balky elevators, shabby dorms, and broken equipment. Student Life complained that university Operational Services were too slow in responding; that they simply placed too low a priority on this work. And in truth, the skilled Ops Services staff did believe that the dorm work was a bit beneath them. They complained that the students were responsible for most of the dorm trashing (such as jammed elevator doors and frequent false fire alarms).

On hearing of the complaints, the University Vice President for Operational Services offered to take over total dormitory operation. He argued that he would run them as hotels with more frequent cleaning, quick maintenance, and ejection of residents who mistreated the facilities.

The Student Life staff `reacted in horror to the Ops Services offer. They feared that all of the social and educational programs that they conducted would be lost in an over-zealous focus on cleaning and discipline.

My inclination was go with Operations Services' proposal. I thought many of the social programs in place were silly. I had a lived in college dorms when the only social programs were student initiated and we wanted no involvement by university staff. Incoming undergraduate students however, increasingly expected a camp-like atmosphere where adult councilors organized their activities. Raised on play dates and adult run little League Baseball, they expected a calendar full of events.

In this debate, Student Affairs pushed the academic card that they reported up the academic hierarchy, that the institution's mission was education, and that their programs contributed to this objective. Operational Services, after all, was just a "service" department.

I recommended a matrix organization like everyone was implementing in the 1980's. Some Operational Services personnel were transferred to Student Life to focus full time on dorm repairs. However, this unit would report up both ladders: to Student Affairs for maintenance and to Ops Services for improvements and skilled maintenance staff promotions. Not one of my more creative solutions.

Unfortunately, drinking and mental health problems have only increased the involvement of university staff in students' lives.

Unearthing the Hidden Millions

At the dawn of the distributed computer age, Digital Electronic Corporation (DEC) sought a foothold in the looming personal computer market. The firm offered to supply us with free Rainbow PC's if we committed to equipment purchases of $20,000,000. Given the size then existing budgets, such a commitment for us would be enormous. We had no idea where we would get the money. But the offer was too attractive to refuse and the agreement was signed.

Surprise. The money came without petitions or prayers. And it didn't come from the university's central administration. Rather like the loaves and fishes, scattered units around the campus recognized the ripeness of the time and investments were made from discretionary funds that had been squirreled away for unknown future uses. The wisdom of dispersed decision-making and the value of some budgetary slack were revealed.

As I gained more administrative experience, I discovered the potential in undetected and perhaps undetectable money hidden in dispersed accounts. Our budgets were of the drop-dead variety; any funds not expended by June 30 were lost. This sometimes led to wasteful spending as the budget year-end approached. But careful planning would allow prepayments for supplies and equipment that experience indicated would be needed in the future. The department's annual Christmas party was a fixture for which I accumulated a prepaid credit for three years in advance. Such a credit balance created some flexibility to respond to unanticipated opportunities without asking for more money. And not bugging the Dean or President brought some political clout.

Too much surplus brought unwarranted attention however. I was once dunned by a Dean for a $40,000 "voluntary" contribution to his office budget. My department was promised interest and repayment, but I saw it as rather like a political campaign contribution. It was not tax deductible.

No Rupert Murdoch I

On the eve of the annual Parents Weekend, the student daily newspaper had published a particularly frightening article about campus crime. Unfortunately, the facts were correct, but the article's lurid tone a bit sensational. At a university Trustees meeting, one trustee associated with the newspaper industry asked why the President didn't just seize all the copies and shut down the paper.

All the university administrators in the room were shocked into silence. We were stunned. Bitter experience had taught us that interfering with the paper would be a public relations disaster probably provoking student demonstrations and sit-in. Besides, it would have been illegal. Similar situations in the past had resulted in total financial and editorial separation between school and paper. We paid for any official university notices as a form of advertising. Otherwise the paper was completely self-supporting. It was not a channel for the administration to communicate with the campus.

A monthly newsletter called *The Gazette* also existed. It was the official university publication for notices of record. And the president could publish personal statements in it (usually then balanced by a faculty oriented interpretation by the Chairperson of the Faculty Senate). The *Gazette* was essentially by and for faculty as it was governed by a faculty editorial committee.

In my opinion, what was missing was a weekly publication aimed at the shared concerns of all university staff as employees. So my colleagues and I started a tabloid sized *The Penn Paper*. It reported current campus news, official personnel notices and presented popular reports on faculty research for all support and professional staff. Space was provided for articles on noteworthy individual accomplishments along with personal announcements. It was a classy newspaper.

Nonetheless, it died rather quickly. Faculty apathy and outright resistance surprised us. Campus activists were particularly skeptical of the administration's intentions (yes, we did want to put a more positive spin on the campus community). Plus, the larger body of faculty just didn't want to think of themselves as employees. The newspaper seemed to lump them together with library aids, maintenance workers, and dining service attendants. And indeed it did.

So ended my ambition to become the Rupert Murdoch of the University of Pennsylvania. One faculty leader told me that I was simply too impatient; that change in academia requires time. Even worse, I had not invested time in floating the idea around campus before initiating publication. Alas, all too true.

Why am I Coming to Admire Ronald Reagan?

I wrote this question in my journal fifteen months after becoming university vice president. I had not been a Reagan admirer. Indeed, I admit that I voted for Jimmy Carter and Walter Mondale!

Nonetheless, as I spent the 1980's in administration, I came to appreciate Reagan's leadership style. He clearly represented the major dimensions of transformative leadership: vision (definition of a focused agenda), meaning (effective communication of cultural values and symbols), trust (clarity, predictability, and consistency), and self-regard (acceptance of others in the here and now).

Of course, Reagan, like everyone else, occasionally wandered away from these attributes, but they represent factors with which academic leaders must repeatedly deal in a period of single issue politics that threaten to fracture the campus community. In the midst of a particularly messy controversy regarding the use of animals in medical research, we had organized a large alumni gathering in Los Angeles. Over 500 alumni turned out for a gala reception at the Chandler Pavilion. Outside, hundreds of animal rights activists were chanting while media-types grilled people under the glare of television lights. It was a bit like the Academy Awards ceremony, which was to be held later that week in the same space. As I dealt with various small emergencies that arose, an alumna came up to me and said, "You are the most relaxed person I've ever seen."

I assume that my observer was complementing me, but it prompted a later entry in my journal, "Leadership is composed so much of acting: in being calm; not discouraged; of communicating confidence and optimism to colleagues." Lou Cannon subtitled his biography of Reagan, "The Role of a Lifetime." And believe me I was acting that night in L.A. Given this vision of leadership and acting, one can understand why Reagan and I both shared a boyhood hero, perhaps the most consummate actor ever to occupy the oval office: Franklin D. Roosevelt.

Of course, dramaturgy is not unknown to good teaching. But the central ethos of academia is open-minded debate about uncertainty. We admire the scholar who can maintain ambivalence until persuasive data are in hand. Leaders, however, often don't have the luxury of time when confronting with divisive issues that are generating anger and anxiety among the university community. They must simply act on a problem, make a decision, and convey a certainty that will persuade prospective followers. Dean Acheson, Harry Truman's Secretary of State, observed in his memoirs that HST was the most decisive person ever to be President in his ability to confront a problem, make a decision, and move on, not being consumed by doubt about his selection.

Truman himself wrote that it never took him more than ten minutes to fall asleep any night that he was in the White House. This suggests either decisiveness or an empty brain depending on one's political posture.

I often admired Truman along with Reagan as I tossed and turned in bed after a day of particularly nettlesome problems.

Wandering the Campus with Vartan

I once had the privilege of serving as Faculty Assistant to Vartan Gregorian when he was Provost of the University of Pennsylvania. Gregorian went on to become a legend as President in turn of The New York Public Library, Brown University, and the Carnegie Corporation. Greg would have multiple ideas every day, which he would jot down and then pull out of his pocket as a crumpled nearly illegible note asking me to investigate and make a recommendation. I would dutifully do so in my straightforward engineering like manner (I had been educated as a mechanical engineer).

Greg would subsequently praise me for my diligence, but suggest that maybe I was too direct and politically insensitive in my approach. He observed that I saw time as Newton's arrow, but that he preferred to see it as a helix or gyre ever widening. Rather than merely solving problems, he saw his role as expanding the ways that people visualize the institution's possibilities. Rather than directing activities, the best leaders emphasize broadening and raising people's aspirations for the institution.

Gregorian seemed generally pleased with my assistance, even to the extent of promising to make me his Provost when he became President of Stanford University (which seemed to be his dream). Greg's critics labeled him as deceitful because he had made similar promises to others. But I never took his praise as literal. Rather the "promise" was simply his way of giving his highest spontaneous praise – by linking you to his dream. He raised a subordinate's aspiration by linking you to his ultimate aspiration. It was simply a metaphor.

Some years later after Gregorian had left Penn, his son and mine were graduating so we marched together in the academic procession. As we wended our way across the campus toward Franklin Field, repeatedly bystanders would step in to greet and embrace Greg as a long lost friend. The hugs came from people as varied as senior chaired professors, to secretaries, to the man who handed out the towels in the gym. When I asked him, Gregorian replied that they were all friends he made a point of chatting with as he had moved around the campus during his time as professor and provost. I observed that you must have spent little time in your office. "As little as possible was his reply."

Clearly, Vartan Gregorian had been moving along his helix developing the multitude of connections that enabled him to build the action coalitions necessary for leadership.

Dining with Athol Fugard

I once enjoyed the distinct honor of sitting at dinner with the famed South African playwright-actor Athol Fugard. We talked about writing. He surprised me by saying that he couldn't write and act at the same time. That is, he had to segment his life between the two. Acting was so energy draining that he simply couldn't summon up his creative juices to write. Writing, however, demanded unbroken concentration for extended periods. He told me about Charles Dickens' strategy for focusing writing time: Dickens would host a party to announce to the world that he was beginning a book and would not be socially available until it was finished. When finished, he would host another party to rejoin the world. Fugard said he alternated years: a year of acting to earn the funds to then withdraw for a year or more of writing.

When Edward Bloustein was named President of Rutgers University, he announced that he intended to continue his legal and pubic policy research, albeit it on a reduced basis. When I asked Sheldon Hackney, Penn's President, whether he thought Bloustein's plan was feasible, Hackney responded with a strong negative. Such career segmentation is just not possible. The administrative, political, and social demands on a university president are just so great that one can't meet them without total investment. Becoming a president in academe is a bit like taking holy orders.

Under such demands, it is difficult to even read anything not task related. After Henry Kissinger left his Harvard professorship to join Richard Nixon's White House staff as National Security Adviser, he wrote that he had to operate on his past knowledge accumulation; there was simply no time to read and talk enough to add new knowledge. So it is for today's university presidents.

Nicholas Murray Butler was president of Columbia University for forty-three years. Obviously that will never be topped. Even more obsolete is that Butler was a famous public intellectual called on by the press to comment on events of the day. Today's university leaders are often criticized for being invisible by not exercising leadership on contemporary matters. It is difficult to find the time and energy. Perhaps more fundamentally, they fear offending one or more of the constituencies on which they are so dependent for attracting students, publishing research and contributing money.

The only college presidency for which I made it as one of the final two candidates disappeared when at a meeting with the trustees I pushed the idea of more students being educated for public service so they could make seamless transitions between private and public enterprise.. One trustee (I assume a conservative – he was a Dartmouth graduate) accused me right there of being a "socialist." For my candidacy, it was a kiss of death.

In retrospect, however, it was a lucky break because I remained free to segment my life ala Fugard's example.

Not Following my own Advice

On New Year's Eve five days after accepting an invitation to become Penn's Vice President for Development and University Affairs, I wrote some resolutions in my journal:

> Don't worry about spending university money.
>
> Delegate; insist that others do it.
>
> Do it my way; don't worry what others think.
>
> I'm, not striving for higher position; relax; don't worry about image or impressing people.
>
> Can't work all the time; pace yourself; get a locker in the gym and work out.

I never had any difficulty with the first item (as my president could too easily testify). Having been an impecunious teacher for so long, I had been concerned that I would be reluctant to spend money even when necessary. I needn't have worried.

I experienced less success with the other reminders. I found myself working most of the time, thinking, if not worrying, about what others might think of me and the university. When I was especially tired, I fell victim to that most pernicious of managerial illusions: that I could do certain tasks better and faster than others to whom they might be delegated. Worst of all, all too soon I was driven by a desire to become president myself. I should have heeded Lord Acton's famous warning about the corruptive effect of power.

I probably worked as many hours per week as a professor, but V.P. life was so different. Most days on campus were divided into half-hour and one-hour meetings scheduled back to back. Lunches were invariable working ones. More often than not, evenings included some university event at which my presence was expected. And weekend football and basketball games were an imperative. And horror of horror, breakfast meetings were proliferating like "want a ride home" signs on holiday campus bulletin boards.

As a professor, I enjoyed much more time freedom. I could work very early or late (more frequently the latter). On the spur of the moment, I could take an afternoon off and go to the museum if my writing muse had temporarily forsaken me – perhaps to return while sitting in the Egyptian gallery. Often this meant working through the weekend if the words were flowing.

As a vice president, the sheer pace of the travels and meetings left me exhausted by weekends and much more protective of them than formerly. It was absolutely essential that I have at least five Sunday hours to catch up on the paperwork that accumulated during the week. Unless I could go into the office on Monday morning with a pile of letters and reports ready for typing, all of the ensuing week would be an uphill struggle.

My ultimate failure to follow my own advice is evident in the last recommendation to myself. I got the gym locker, but in five years didn't open it even once!

III
Cultivating Alumni
and
Raising Money

Roughing it in Palm Beach

Someone had to go. Every February required a cultivation trip visiting alumni in Palm Beach and Boca Raton. It might as well be me. This usually meant putting up with the hardships of the Boca Raton Club with its pink stucco Moorish architecture and luxuriant gardens. But I sacrificed for good old Penn. Indeed some of our alumni sacrificed with me. I was having lunch with a wonderful university friend when gesturing enthusiastically about Penn events I knocked over his wine glass spilling a rich red Cabernet all over his lovely white silk suit. And he still made a gift.

Of course, many alumni wealthy enough to afford homes in Palm Beach had their peccadilloes. I talked about a possible gift with an elderly alumnus who had graduated in the 1920's. He was very gracious, and showed me around his fantastic penthouse in the Breakers before lunch was served. I knew his net worth was in the high millions so I was seeking at least an endowed professorship in his name (about 1.5 million dollars then). He committed to a nice gift, but not in that ballpark. As he explained, he would not make a gift out of "principal" because he didn't want to run out of funds before he died. He was 93 at the time! Now, that is optimism.

Not giving out of principal was especially true of widows. However much many wanted to honor their late husbands' love of *alma mater*, they were loath to make a gift that would reduce the funds on which they drew to live. No illustration of this being impossible was persuasive.

Not every alumnus in Florida was old. Some were entrepreneurs who had made their fortunes early. I met with the owner of national chain of jewelry stores and requested a gift of $10,000. He looked at me with distain, asking didn't I know that for him such a small amount was chicken feed. I quickly added that I meant $10,000 per year as a member of our highest Annual Giving group. But, he clearly felt insulted that my expectation wasn't much higher. Unhappily, I never even got what I asked for.

I remember a particularly lovely reception and dinner we gave at a private Lake Worth estate. While sipping cocktails next to the pool I was reminded of one of the most famous scenes in cinema history. In "The Graduate," Dustin Hoffman's character Benjamin has just graduated from college when he seeks advice from a guest at his parent's poolside party. He is told "Plastics, my boy, there's a real future in plastics." Well, I was long since past college graduation, but in Palm Beach at that party in 1984 mobile phone entrepreneur George Lindemann told me, "Cell phones, Ross, cell phones are the future."

I didn't have any idea what a cell phone was or why anyone would want one. I could only envision one possible use – as an emergency aid for old people. I doubt that even my cell phone investment advisor imagined how the technology would become a sub teen's umbilical cord. Needless to say, I didn't make an investment.

At evening's end after all the guests had left, I was sitting with the hostess, who had consumed a few too many gin and tonics. She proceeded to confide that she was disappointed that she had never been allowed any say in the furniture and decorations in her *Architectural Digest* home. She just didn't feel it was her house because all decisions were made by her mother-in-law. And her husband wouldn't stand up to his mother.

See, inheritance is not all that it's cracked up to be. Even the rich have problems.

California Dreaming

Road warriors like salespersons and management consultants take pride in mastering a new territory. Learning where to eat and how to drive on the freeways around Los Angeles is a particular challenge. It is satisfying being able to drive from Malibu to Santa Monica and on to Central City or La Brea, etc. Most exciting, however, was driving up Mullholland Drive and surveying the Valley spread out below. David Lynch's film *Mullholland Drive* brought back memories.

But then *Pretty Woman* also brought back memories because Michael Milken's office was located on Wilshire at the foot of Rodeo Drive. At the time he was running the California office of Drexel Burnham Lambert, which had created a whole new market in high risk and convertible securities (junk bonds). I called on Michael in his custom designed office where he sat in the center of a semi-circle of computer monitors displaying market activity around the world. His multitasking skill was certainly impressive. His eyes continually scanned his screens while conversing in a very knowledgeable way about Penn's needs. He became one of the most thoughtful and creative of our donors giving special attention to the social and physical development of West Philadelphia.

A highlight (or lowlight) of that trip was attending the luncheon during his annual "Predator's Ball" where financial investors from around the world gathered to hear of Milken's latest proposals. I was seated at a table with Saul Steinberg and Ivan Bolsky, both of whom eventually suffered significant legal and financial difficulties. How lucky I was not to be a big investor.

If Milken represented the epitome of California new money, the Mudd Foundation was synonymous with old. I met with the last two living foundation trustees in the even more elderly and stuffy California Club. The trustee chairman looked exactly like Ralph Bellamy in the film *Changing Places*. He committed to a gift, but unfortunately their regulations limited gifts to only new buildings that would bear the Mudd name. And they only had $1 million left for this would be their last gift. What could we build for only one million?

Actually, Penn's Plant Science soon benefited from a lovely greenhouse housing thousands of experimental plants. We brought a little California greenery to brighten West Philadelphia.

Jack Welch's Empty Building

The ride in the limo was the first since my wedding. General Electric had sent it the train station in Stanford to convey us to GE's Fairfield, Connecticut headquarters. Along with Russ Palmer the Dean of the Wharton School, I was calling on the new Chief Executive Officer Jack Welch. We were met at the front door by one of his secretaries who graciously guided us through a very large and quite empty first floor.

When I asked her about all the non-occupied offices and desks, she remarked: "You should have seen it when Mr. Jones was here; it was very full then!"

Mr. Jones was Reginald Jones, a Wharton and Penn alumnus who had been Jack Welch's predecessor as General Electric's C.E.O. We were visiting to discuss G.E.'s support for the Jones Center and Professorship at Jones's *alma mater.* Reg had been a loyal supporter having served as a trustee and chairman of its development committee. He had also been the Business Roundtable's most admired business CEO of the 1970's (as Welch was to be in the 80's and 90's).

I was a little concerned that Welch would be aware that recently I had served as an expert witness in defense of a GE sub-contractor who had claimed that GE's unrealistic budget pressure had justified its not informing the

U.S. Defense Department of some unexpected cost savings in a contract. Federal law requires a contractor to inform the government if unanticipated cost savings arise during the course of a contract. The sub-contractor didn't report some of these because, they argued, doing so would have made it impossible to meet GE's expectations. I hadn't agreed with their violating the law, but did feel that GE's pressure was too inflexible. Luckily, Welch was not aware of the case.

Given that Jones took pride in his nominating Welch as his replacement, I was surprised at Welch's implicit criticism of Jones' management. He commented on the need to reduce corporate staff and to push more of these duties onto operating managers with profit and loss responsibilities. Jones' corporate strategic planning staff had been one of the most prestigious positions in American business for newly graduating MBA's. Welch had reduced it by ninety percent. In addition, Welch said that unlike his predecessor he was not going to spend a lot of time courting federal politicians and bureaucrats in Washington, D.C. His focus was going to be on reducing cost and improving operating efficiencies.

Results proved the validity of Welch's decisions for the challenges he confronted. Total return to shareholders was a cumulative 1400 percent for the twenty years in which he served as CEO.

Still, as I left our meeting and walked back through the eerily empty building, I understood why Welch came to be nicknamed "Neutron Jack" after the so-called neutron bomb. The buildings remained, but the people were gone.

Strange Rendezvous

Most meetings with potential donors were in offices, some in homes, but a few others took place in strange locations.

At 7:00 am on a wintry morning I met with a former student of mine in the bowels of Chicago's Southside in a MacDonald's that he owned. I had my first ever egg Mac Muffin there – and it was good. Unhappily, my former student was in tight financial straits and a bit too aggressive as an entrepreneur. He was later imprisoned and charged with attempted murder of a competitor.

From the south side I traveled to the loop to meet in the office of the architects Skidmore, Owens Merrill on the 100th floor of the Sears tower. The transition literally made me sea (air?) sick from the building's swaying in the legendary Chicago wind. Sick, but not afraid because I was meeting with alumnus Bruce Graham who had designed the building. Surely it was safe if his office was up there.

With the stock market boom of the 1980's, many alumni in financial services dreamed of amassing enough money to retire early, raise Black Angus cattle in upstate New York as a tax write off, and **LIVE** the rest of their lives for enjoyment. The dreams were never viable for most, but enough did it to feed the myth. I met one alumnus who was leading the dream. He met with me on a beach in Venice, California. His passion was woman's volleyball and he was commissioner of a professional league. At our meeting we were literally surrounded by bouncing bikini clad beautiful women, all, it seemed to me, over six feet tall. Amazingly, he made a generous gift of over a million dollars to endow a chair in the name of a finance professor whom he admired. I could readily see why he was so grateful for his financial acumen.

Another successful investor met me in an exercise facility that he had built both for himself and as a research laboratory. He was sponsoring physiologists and therapists to explore whether males over forty-five or so through exercise could still add muscle mass. While he was pumping away, I made my pitch to preserve his legacy through a meaningful gift to his alma mater. Alas, he seemed more interested in simply preserving his own body.

Unfortunately, I am only five foot eight inches and was never very good at volleyball – and I didn't start lifting weights until I was over sixty years of age so no noticeable muscle growth is evident.

The Dreams of a Twenty-Two Year Old

Two Penn alumni Bill Novelli and Jack Porter founded one of the most creative public relations firms in Washington, D.C. Jack was very helpful to me during various P.R. tribulations and Bill has gone on to be President of the AARP.

They possessed exceptional insight into the post Vietnam era young adults which is reflected in a magazine advertisement recruiting for their own firm. A young mid 20ish woman is pictured sitting on the beach with her laptop computer. The copy asks, "What do you want?" Underneath is a "quotation" about what she is thinking:

> "I want to write my own ticket. High tech is a wide-open field. I'm helping to create public relations programs for companies that are on the leading edge of software development. What I'm learning is making one fabulous career. I want to hit the beach. I grew up on the West Coast. The Ocean has always been my second home. Whenever I need to think things through, this is where I come. I want to keep climbing. Each year my role gets bigger. My managers support my growth with professional development

> and mentoring programs. It's like being back in college. I want to go to Africa. Next year I hope. (Incidentally, our health insurance plan is great). I want to be the best. If there's a limit to what I'm capable of achieving, I'm not sure where it is or when I'll reach it. Never, I hope."

I often used this advertisement with my executive education groups seeking their response to the attitude expressed. Not surprisingly (to me at least) many if not most of the middle-aged and older managers (predominantly men) were quite offended by the young lady's thoughts, "Unrealistic," "Self-centered," and "immature" are among the labels thrown out in class. Not a little intergenerational envy and anger were voiced.

Being near the end of my career, I can certainly understand the older managers' reservations what the young woman in the ad represented. And yet, as I look back over the years it is striking how I was able to do virtually all the things she aspired to. So perhaps she isn't as unrealistically idealistic as she appears to people in mid-life when life's demands and routines are most pressing.

I see little in the life motivations of today's twenty-two year olds that is much different than what today's senior citizens were wishing for fifty years ago.

My Date with Imelda Marcos

Imelda Marcos had a graduate student son at Penn so it was normal that she would want to visit the campus. Unfortunately, she came with an entourage expecting it to be a state visit including a presidential dinner in her honor. This created a campus political dilemma. Given the attacks on the autocratic and ethical climate of the Marcos administration in the Philippines, her presence on campus would be sure to elicit significant opposition with accompanying photogenic demonstrations. And naturally we did not want to provoke political anger among state legislators that might provoke cuts in certain state appropriations.

So the university grand Pooh-Bahs put their collective wisdom together and decided that neither the President nor Provost should be seen in pictures with Mrs. Marcos. Therefore, neither could host or appear at any public function. So I, as Faculty Assistant to the President, was given the dubious honor of hosting a luncheon for our guest, not on campus, but at a downtown club.

When the great day of our blind date arrived, Imelda swept in accompanied by her followers and camera crew that captured every minute of our conversation. She must have been aware of the snub that she had received, but she was all graciousness and treated me if as I were the President of the United States. I couldn't help but sneak a look at her shoes to see which of the thousands that she was reputed to own she had selected for me. They were a lovely silk magenta.

Now I must admit that our luncheon was quite delightful. Imelda was very attractive (I was even a little disconcerted because she actually resembled my mother in her beauty and friendliness). Plus I always wondered when watching news films of state dinners what the diners actually talked about. We talked of Broadway Shows. She adored Stephen Sondheim.

As our luncheon neared an end, however, I began to worry that she was going to invite me up to her room for an after meal drink. Indeed, I was beginning to feel like a mouse being eyed by a crouching cat. Like many more or less presentable men, I had my share of illusions about my attractiveness, but I hardly wanted any hint of involvement with the wife of a near all-powerful dictator.

Pleading the pressures of time, I fled back to my College Hall sanctuary and the safer world of campus rather than international politics.

She never called for another date.

Two Paths Diverged in the City

Renowned investor Warrant Buffet recently was quoted as saying half of what business schools teach is nonsense. But which half? Distinguishing between the two parts is impossible. Even though Buffet spent less than a full freshman year at Penn, I like to assume that the nonsense is what he learned at his later schools (judiciously unnamed here).

Many of our alumni, like Buffet, pursued careers in investments and financial services. One of the most impressive was Michael Tarnopol, late Vice Chairman of both Bear Stearns and the University Trustees. Mickey's Penn legacy was dramatically represented in his office by the red and blue oar that he stroked as a member of the crew.

Although thought to be a glamorous destination for new graduates, the early years on Wall Street are very tough in hours and foregone social life. Worse, many tasks are just boring numbers crunching. Worst of all, many financial services managers are just poor managers. They tend to be self-centered, overly ambitious, and insensitive to subordinates. For most of their lives they were rewarded for personal achievement rather than team accomplishments. Consequently, money becomes the primary incentive for people to stay long enough until they finally get interesting work. An investment banker explained to me the three elements in getting a young person hooked on the earning potential on Wall Street:

> "Get them married: this dramatically increases the need for money and reduces the time for social life.
>
> Get them to buy a Manhattan apartment: this locks them into high monthly mortgage and real estate tax payments reducing personal freedom to quit.
>
> Most powerfully, get them to buy a vacation home in the Hamptons: now the financial commitments are so high that a by then slightly more mature associate will do most anything to preserve his bonus."

With apology to Robert Frost, which is the path less chosen that could make all the difference? A stairway to Easthampton heaven or a primrose path to Wall Street hell?

Terry Gross and the Angry Trustee

For over twenty years, Terry Gross has been one of the finest interviewers in America. Her National Public Radio show *Fresh Air* has demonstrated her incredible talent in earning the trust of her guests and thus eliciting exceptional candor. Back when she was a local Philadelphia show, I had the pleasure of being her guest in a discussion of time management. She had more knowledge of my own book than I did.

When *Fresh Air* was proposing to go national, as Vice President responsible for media relations, I was asked whether Penn might be interested in making a contribution in support of the additional promotional expenses. In return, the university would receive a credit, "This broadcast is brought to you by the generous support of the University of Pennsylvania, etc." I allocated a $10,000 donation to WHYY Radio's effort.

Unhappily, I was quickly chastised by a senior University Trustee for what he considered unseemly advertising. He felt it was inappropriate for a university to do so – especially using money that donors had contributed to the institution. To buttress my argument, I showed him some Harvard advertisements, but I'm afraid that only validated his opinion. Now, this was long before most universities, especially their medical centers, had begun to advertise through multiple media including large billboards on the Walt Whitman Bridge. So when the initial grant ran out, I didn't renew it and we missed the nationwide promotional push that being allied with Terry Gross would have provided.

My thoughts then and now turn to my late Penn colleague Digby Baltzell's famous book about Philadelphia reticence and Boston aggressiveness in his *Quaker Philadelphia and Puritan Boston.*

Betting Admissions Chips

White waiting in line to renew my driver's license at the New Jersey Motor Vehicle office, an alumnus introduced me to his high school son as "Mr. Pennsylvania – the man who could get you into Penn."

Although more brazen than most, this alumnus acquaintance was not alone. I received many inquiries asking that I support a candidate's application. In most cases I tried to meet with the potential student so I at least didn't have to lie on a recommendation letter. I would generally write a letter ranging from neutral to strong enthusiasm based upon my admittedly superficial acquaintanceship. This was no different than any faculty member would do.

As Vice President for Development and University Relations, however, I was in a different status. I had to consider the school's long-range institutional interests. Were there important political or financial implications to be factored in?

Upon hearing from an alumnus VIP regarding a candidate (most frequently, his or her child), I would try to get the parent to honestly assess the academic strengths of their child. Did they really think that she would be able to handle Penn's pressure? Would he be happy here? Having to subsequently leave would be greater trauma than not being accepted. Sometimes this would persuade the VIP parent to reconsider their child's application. But, usually not.

If not, I could have a problem. I had a limited number of slots which I could strongly influence – like the football coach. I tried to allocate them fairly to optimize the university's financial, political, and social interests. What had been the parents' contributions history? (Past gifts, not promised future ones). I was rarely asked point blank "how large a gift would it take?" (although it happened). No amount was the answer. But giving history did count as did political support and alumni service.

I normally couldn't meet all VIP desires so I had to prioritize. Among the finalists, the first pass was my assessment of their academic promise. That is, even though the sons or daughters was not as academically strong as most Penn applicants, who had the best chance of succeeding?

This meant that every year I had to call some important university friends to tell that their child had little chance of being accepted. Perhaps their little darling should apply elsewhere. Not all were happy to hear this, of course, but a surprising number seemed genuinely relieved that their child would not be starting a program that they would likely fail. I had relieved the parents of continued pushing. They felt they had done their duty,

Unhappily, every year I ended up with a couple or so children of wealthy donors or political stalwarts who simply would not accept that their child wasn't (as at Lake Woebegone) "well above average." I did receive some "I'll never make another gift" letters.

Even Ivy League Schools have flunkouts. But I sure wish I had a two percent cut on the current incomes of some of the weaker candidates I interviewed!

Revenge of the Disappointed Alumnus

The handling of an alumni child's undergraduate application is the most influential determinant of the parents' subsequent attitude toward the university – especially their willingness to contribute money. When I was Penn's chief fundraiser, my staff asked me to call on a Western Pennsylvania alumnus who appeared to have significant unrealized giving potential. Somehow in my briefing I didn't note that his two sons had been rejected by Penn a total of four times! Failed applications included the College of Arts and Sciences, the Wharton School, The Law School and the Medical School. It was one of my less successful visits.

For good or ill, many schools give some additional weight to an applicant's "legacy." Nonetheless, many alumni children are rejected. How this is communicated is critical. A personal on-campus interview for all applicants is not feasible at schools that receive thousands of applications. But it is essential for alumni children in order to shape the frame of reference for a future possible rejection. After the admission office decision, an advance telephone call with the negative (or positive) result is desirable to maintain good relations with the alumni parents.

Like many other parents, I had a child rejected by my *alma mater,* Princeton University. It was even more disappointing because of their miscommunication. My daughter was a highly recruited high school field hockey and lacrosse player. She was tops on the Princeton coach's desired list, but the coach decided not to expend an admission chip on Jennifer because of the assumption that she would be admitted as a legacy child. Unhappily, my clout was insufficient.

So Jennifer enrolled at Penn from where she graduated in four years after an outstanding athletic career achieving All-Ivy status in two sports. One of the highlights of my years at Penn occurred when in a freshman lacrosse game against Princeton. Jennifer alone scored eight goals while the orange and black as a team scored only seven. This was followed by almost as good a feeling when I as Penn's Vice President for Development enjoyed seeing us pass Princeton for the first time in total gifts received.

Not every disappointed alumnus parent has the same opportunities for revenge.

What Alumni are the Most Loyal?

Henry Ford reputedly once said: "all history is bunk!" History may be erroneous, but it is real and never really past. Nowhere is this more evident than in the attitudes that alumni bring to their undergraduate memories.

Unrestricted gifts to Annual Giving are one of the best indicators of alumni feelings. The percentage of alumni who contribute is especially sensitive to loyalty. Among the Ivy-MIT-Stanford group that exchange data on such matters, Princeton and Dartmouth usually elicit the highest percentage of alumni contributing – generally attributed to their somewhat smaller enrollment, more isolated locale and long-time (until the 1970s) all male status. The larger more urban located schools such as Harvard and Penn tend to have a lower contribution percentage – attributed to students having more social alternatives and less involvement in the campus.

At Penn we explored the relationship between undergraduate activities and subsequent inclination to contribute money. Among the sport teams, football alumni generally contributed the least and crew the most. Academic and socio-economic factors undoubtedly play a role here, but in general, the football players in their prime giving years felt that they had essentially given years ago when they played. Plus, the older ones were still angry because 40 years previously, Penn had deemphasized football, dropping athletic scholarships and games against national powerhouses like Notre Dame and Michigan. They were not excited about games with Columbia and Brown. By the early 1960's, things had been become so bad that the late, great Frank Dolson, alumnus and former Sports Editor of the *Philadelphia Inquirer*, as a young reporter attended all Penn football practices just to observe commitment to a hopeless cause, a pure exercise in amateur futility.

In contrast, crew remained a national power because it had always been mainly a non-scholarship, amateur sport loved by parochial and private school graduates. Plus, the rower's commitment must be extraordinary to put up with the virtually year round early morning workouts. Sticking with it develops strong loyalty to the university.

The same argument applies to another activity that produces high loyalty: work on the undergraduate student newspaper, *The Daily Pennsylvanian*. This was quite surprising to me because the newspaper is traditionally not shy about criticizing the administration for its failings. But this criticism seems to grow out of caring about the institution. And the enormous time commitment that goes into editing the paper leads to adult loyalty. Those undergrads who participate little and drift through four years tend to be the same in later years.

The University of Pennsylvania's rise in charitable gifts received during the 1980's owed much to a particularly faithful group of alumni: Jewish graduates of the 1950's and 60's. It is generally credited to Penn that it was the first of the Ivy League colleges to eliminate the quota system for Jewish applicants. It is not clear whether this was a conscious policy decision or simply a response to the quality of applicants. Surely, Penn's Quaker origins encouraged it to seek out and recognize talent whatever its origins. The result is that by the time these graduates reached a life stage where they were able to make significant gifts, their *alma mater* was a fortunate recipient.

Shrugging off Atlas's Gift

A wealthy Ayn Rand admirer offered to donate millions to endow a professorship and program in "Objectivism." A successful alumnus entrepreneur, he was disturbed by what he considered the school's excessive focus on teamwork. In response to employers' criticism that our graduates were very ambitious and analytically talented, but inept in working with others, we recast the curriculum to emphasize more teamwork and learning how to lead by learning how to follow. Big corporations applauded our reemphasis, but many small business entrepreneurs judged it absolutely wrong. They considered themselves to be strong individualists who would not have made it being more "team" oriented. They wanted us to reinforce their individualistic attitudes – hence their admiration for Rand.

Our donor wanted to name the professorship for his late father who had started as an itinerant merchant. Surely, a laudable intention. But he wanted the program to "promote" objectivism and its economic policy implications. The university could not accept such a constrained mission. Objectivism as a philosophy certainly can be discussed in a balanced analysis of individualism, capitalism, communalism, and socialism, but not advanced as the path to success. We could and did discuss the differing personalities of corporate hierarchy climbers and new enterprise founders. No serious academic institution, however, can accept contributions with a propagandistic agenda. It would undermine the school's reputation as a scholarly enterprise.

Even accepting gifts more aligned to the university's ethos can be dangerous if too much program control is ceded to the donor. One wanted to underwrite a research program that should "show" how NASA contributed to American's technological development. I explained that we would love to mount a project evaluating the positive and negative effects of the space program along with the economic costs and benefits. He had no interest in such academic research.

Time passes. A gift's original intention may no longer fit institutional priorities or society's needs may have changed. We need sufficient flexibility to redirect funds in ways that are hopefully congenial with the original purpose, but more contemporary with current needs. Unhappily, some donors (especially those who had an original ideological agenda) reject such flexibility. In recent years both Yale and Princeton have had to return funds or settle with unhappy donors who felt their original objectives were being ignored or distorted. One famous businessman once donated what we considered a "token" (for his wealth) gift of $5000 toward a fund to help us retain a very successful football coach. When the coach left for more challenging pastures, however, our fair weather alumnus asked for his money back.

That request was easy to shrug off.

My First (and Only) $1,000,000,000 Check

I was in Martin Lipton's office at the Wall Street Law firm, Wachtell and Lipton, when he allowed me to hold a billion dollar check from Texaco that was part of the payoff in the Texaco-Pennzoil dispute over Getty Oil. Alas, it was not made out to the University of Pennsylvania.

We were holding a reception in Lipton's office for alumni in the New York City legal community. We thought that the check combined with the Piper Heidsick might inspire them to make some more modest, but still significant contributions. We were seeking some new supporters to compensate for General Electric's acquisition of RCA. They had constituted our two largest corporate contributors and it was clear that the combined firm would not be giving as much as the two firms separately had done.

Cultivation and courtship of potential donors has long been a staple of university fundraising. What has changed over the years has been the additional effort to find a match between the donor's interests and the institution's needs. Entrepreneurs and executive types increasingly seek a clearly defined link between their gifts and world impact. Simply naming a building is a less powerful motivator that creating an innovative program that matches the donor's values with society's needs.

Lacking faith that the administration will use their money wisely, many donors refrain from making large unrestricted gifts. Ideological differences sometimes lead to distrust; donors suing the school for alleged misuse of funds is not uncommon. Consequently, it is imperative that university leadership carefully assesses a potential donor's interest, and presents to him or her a creative set of initiatives; there is little interest in repairing buildings that are falling down.

Often university leaders need to pursue a substantial educational effort to convince donors that priorities have changed. The Ivy League transition from merit scholarships to financial aid based on need was a particular challenge. Alumni from the 1930's to 1950's were familiar with scholarships based on the applicant's academic promise rather than financial need. Many high potential applicants from past years of course needed scholarships to attend, but the essential orientation was demonstrated academic performance.

In the laudable desire to foster more racial, ethnic, and economic diversity among students, the Ivy group (and many other colleges of course) changed to need blind admissions in which the financial aid decision was made separately after the admission decision. Scholarships and loans were offered to the students needing financial need, even if they showed less academic potential than some of the admitted students from more affluent families.

This transition was difficult for older alumni to support. When we began to seek funds for sharply expanded need-based scholarships, we initially met resistance from those who thought we were abandoning the merit concept. Some even complained that we had initiated a double standard, giving more money to less qualified students than to the more qualified. Thankfully, in time potential donors came to understand that the long-term interests of their colleges and the nation were better served by recognizing the obstacles that a more diverse student body encountered in attending.

In a perverse way the wide recognition of the need for financial aid endowments grew with the greater than inflation rate of increase in tuition, room and board. More and more applicants simply could not afford us.

In retrospect, it is a bit quaint to realize that Texaco's billion-dollar check was written on paper rather than an electronic transfer.

Glitter at the New York Stock Exchange

At the height of Drexel Burnham Lambert's highflying trajectory in the 1980's, Penn gave a party for all of our alumni employees. The roster of successful and wealthy alumni included I.W. Burnham, Jon Burnham, and Michael Milken. Hurrahs and toasts filled the air. I was thrilled to sit in the director's chair assigned to Laurence Tisch, then Chairman of CBS where my father had worked for so many years. And as head of Penn's fundraising, I keenly anticipated the flow of gifts that we hoped to elicit from those drinking the champagne.

Alas, in short order the firm's star felt along with Milken and more than a few alumni found their careers in tatters. No simple explanation answers all the questions. Some argue that individuals and the firm were treated unfairly; that in fact innovations like the packaging of junk bonds was a positive contribution to financial markets. Surely brains were not in short supply. After meeting Milken, Penn's president Sheldon Hackney told me that Michael was one of the smartest persons he had ever met.

I have gained some insight into the ethical woes of recent years based on data collected back in the 70's and 80's. It was striking then how more pessimistic undergrads and MBA students were about business ethics than were senior executives. And how much more cynical the students were about the behavior of others in problematic situations. It added up to lower self-standards than older and experienced managers voiced.

The pessimism and cynicism of those 20 something students thirty years ago was significantly influenced by the negative views about business that they had heard in high school from teachers then at the height of the anti-authority, anti-organizational mentality from the 1960's and 70's. Now those students are in their late 40's, early 50's, and in charge of corporate America.

Sadly, they appear to lack the optimism, trust in others and mission sense that characterized executives from the 1940's and 50's.

On Feeding White Elephants with Diamonds

Because of its long life and immobility (Penn cannot relocate to the Caribbean, – more's the pity), a successful university can become particularly burdened by past cultural practices and building decisions. A university budget director once explained that the strongest determinant of a department's operating expense was the square footage they occupied. So when Arts and Science faculty complained about the higher salaries paid to Business School faculty, they conveniently overlooked the fact that the latter occupied offices one-quarter the size of the former. Arts and Science faculty tended to be in older classical buildings with large offices while business was in less ambitious post World War II structures. The older buildings were enormously more expensive per faculty member (not to mention that the number of students in business school classes was roughly twice as many as a typical A&S class!). To use a term that is anathema to A&S people, the business school was much more economically efficient.

Massive football stadiums present a common example of how the past limits present decisions. A stadium built to accommodate large crowds during a team's heyday becomes an albatross on the budget when the sport is deemphasized. I well remember when on a job visit to Tulane University coming across the gigantic rusting hulk of a stadium smack in the middle of its campus, long after the school's football fortunes had evaporated. For Penn the stadium is Franklin Field. Actually, Franklin Field is quite beautiful. Resembling an ivy-covered Roman coliseum, it is the oldest double-decked stadium in the country. In its prime, it was home to a top ten college team as well as the Philadelphia Eagles of the NFL. It was routine to host 140,000 fans over a weekend. Old timers still claim it was the best place ever to watch the game because of proximity to the players.

In time, the Eagles flew away to their own venue and the university decided it would rather compete to crash the top ten in academics rather than football. A crowd of 15,000 was about the best we could expect. That left some 55,000 empty seats! Even with reduced attendance, slabs of concrete were a constant threat to rain down on entering and exiting fans. The venerable field was collapsing.

Investigation revealed, to our surprise, that the giant U-shaped coliseum had been built without expansion joints. The contractions and expansions of the Philadelphia weather were tearing it apart. Letting it collapse was too dangerous. Tearing it down seemed more attractive. It could be replaced by a more modern and flexible use 25,000 seat stadium, more than enough capacity for most events (except the Penn Relays which are the only event close to capacity, but that is only two days in April). Princeton tore down its revered Palmer Stadium and replaced it with just such a new facility.

Franklin Field, however, was an icon to Philadelphia and Penn, especially to mature alumni in their peak giving years. They remember the packed stands and exciting games against Notre Dame, Michigan, and Navy among others.

Diamonds came to the rescue. They were imbedded in the hardened steel blades of a giant saw. Twenty-four top to bottom joints were cut in the steel, concrete, and bricks allowing flexibility with the heat and cold. The operation was a success; the stadium survived and is thriving. But whether the operation should have been performed is doubtful. Playing Lafayette, Lehigh and Towson is not all that fan attracting. But those 55,000 empty seats are safer and look better.

Unhappily, some white elephants are so sacred that they demand feeding with expensive food.

Splintered Family Ties

Most of the alumni visits that I made were in their professional or business offices. Business owners and executives were particularly interested to show off their achievements to me as a professor of management in a business school. So I often got to visit factories and offices meeting employees and colleagues.

I especially enjoyed a visit with Lee Bass who was a young Wharton MBA alumnus. I met with him in the Bass family's skyscraper in Forth Worth with its magnificent view of the Texas landscape. Since Lee was a Yale undergraduate alumnus, to make a strong entrance, I wore my PENN BEAT YALE football pin. He was so excited about the pin he immediately walked me down the hall to meet his father, the formidable Perry Bass (also a Yale grad, no connection to Penn). It was an entree never anticipated.

Sometimes, it was more convenient to meet at alumni homes. This could be hazardous. I called on a brilliant alumna of whom we were not aware until her financial and legal success landed her on the cover of a national business magazine. She agreed to see me at home. Upon parking my car and walking up the driveway, I was greeted by her five-year-old son sitting in his electric car who then proceeded to drive right into my legs.

Fighting the pain and hoping not to show my tears, I greeted his mother. Her Lafayette grad husband joked that his wife better watch out now that Penn had finally discovered her. Well, it was a great discovery; she went on to become a major donor and university trustee. My pain was not in vain.

Sometimes relationships became so close that I was invited stay over in private homes. Mike's home in Texas was particularly lovely and his family most gracious. He bore, after all, one of the most prominent names in his industry – real estate development. The mixed residential and commercial developments associated with his family name were staggering in ambition and execution.

It was clear that Mike had a strong desire to care for his family while achieving great aesthetic and financial success. After several years, Mike's success and loyalty to his alma mater brought election to Penn's Board of Trustees. While he was attending one of the board's meetings, we chanced to be walking across Paley College Green together when he earnestly urged me to teach my students the importance of balancing their lives; of not allowing professional ambitions to undermine family ties. He then explained that because he was unable to do so, he had lost his family. The hurt in his heart was palpable.

I certain agreed with his message. I had tried to observe its wisdom in my personal life. Nonetheless, it is doubtful that my advice would have had much impact on unmarried MBA students dreaming of becoming Donald Trump and meeting the next "Mrs. Trump."

Sipping Vodka on Butcher's Block

Howard Butcher was a legend in Penn history. As a trustee, he was chairman of the investment committee responsible for the university's endowment. A Quaker by commitment and a Conservative by inclination, he stuck with the tried and true.

Legend has it that the university was one of the largest owners of the Pennsylvania Railroad since the days of Chairman Alexander Cassett (Mary's brother). Indeed, it is reported that Butcher held on to the stock right up to the firm's bankruptcy in 1970. Like many university endowments which suffered from excessive conservatism, Penn's dramatically declined in real value during the stagnant late 1960's and 1970's.

When the New York Stock Exchange converted from paper chits to computers, the ornate oak trading station for the Pennsy was donated to the Wharton School where it now serves as an impressive bar for entertaining potential donors.

Butcher was chairman of the brokerage and investment banking firm of Butcher and Singer. Its headquarters were on Walnut Street in Philadelphia in a converted majestic bank building. I used to call on Howard in his private space on a large open floor. It was located just to the left of the entrance on a slight rise so he could observe his people at work. He didn't believe in ostentatious expenditures, however, and practically nothing had been done to refurbish the aging space. The furniture was well scratched and the carpet threadbare.

Howard's building today is much transformed. Until recently, the entire room was occupied by one of the city's finest restaurants, Striped Bass. His former office area was the location of a pink marble pillared bar. There was no finer place in town at which to sit sipping a Stoli on the Rocks while contemplating time's transformations.

Certainly ironic for an old Quaker family.

Friendly Cutthroat Competition

We were sitting in a meeting at Harvard when the door opened. In walked a smaller older man with a large dusting glove on his right hand and a small stepladder in his left.. No one stopped him and no one asked his intention. We all sensed it. Without saying a word, very slowly he walked to the large set of windows and began dusting the Venetian blinds one by one. The rest of us looked at each other and wordlessly sighed, "Only at Harvard." Most of the rest of us knew that our blinds would never be cleaned unless we did it ourselves.

In this case, the meeting was of the Vice Presidents and chief development officers of the Ivy-MIT-Stanford group. This group of ten schools meets annually to compare their fundraising performance and how much they spent to raise the donations. The group is exclusive by definition for the ten schools represented see themselves as the most academically competitive private universities in the country. They usually dominate the annual top ten in gifts received.

Each Development Vice President personally announces to the assembled group his or her school's performance for the past year. Everyone politely applauds every announcement, but actually, it is a cut-throat competition. The smaller schools can't expect to top the traditional standbys at the top, but all can compete for the highest productivity as represented by some other appropriate measure such as: (a) the ratio of total dollar gifts pledged divided by the development budget, (b) percentage increase from the previous year, or (c) percentage of living alumni who contributed.

Over the years, Harvard and Yale had more frequently led in total funds raised although other schools in the middle of a major campaign might jump into second place for a short time. Similarly, Dartmouth and Princeton most frequently led in percentage of alumni contributing which reached its peak at about 70 percent. At the time of this Harvard meeting, Stanford and Penn were experiencing the most rapid gift growth.

Who was most efficient in fund raising was a bit harder to decipher. All aimed to spend less than 10 percent of the gifts pledged. The problem was that some of us had budgets that were more transparent than others were. Stanford, MIT, and Cornell with their strong engineering/science emphasis raised relatively more money from corporations than the rest of us. This cost less per dollar received than cultivating and soliciting individual alumni.

The budgets reported for Yale, Princeton and Harvard were, to these eyes at least, a bit suspicious. The Yale development office was allowed to keep some of the funds it raised over its target. This wasn't included in their public budget. Princeton seemed to have an "off the books" supplemental development budget, probably to placate faculty who complained that they spent too much on fund raising.

Rich Harvard couldn't even tell us how much they actually spent. The university was so decentralized and budgets so decoupled that no central officer really knew what the semi-autonomous schools were doing. Their motto was, "Every tub on its own bottom" – meaning that every school had to balance its own budget (by hook or crook some of us thought).

Whatever their means, Harvard and Princeton were in the most attractive financial positions: The Cantabs because in total dollars invested they had the largest endowment; the Tigers whose endowment was the largest in the ratio to the university's size (measured either by number of faculty or students). After attending the first of these IVY-MIT-Stanford meetings, I issued a dictum to my staff that in their budget proposals I would not accept any reference to what they were spending at either Princeton or Harvard!

Shortly after returning to my office, I received a call from John McKay of the University of Southern California. U.S.C. had expressed interest in being included in the Ivy-MIT-Stanford group, which was logical given its academic and fundraising success. But John McKay was not USC's development VP; he was the extremely successful coach of the national champion football team. I think he was a bit bored by his success so he was considering moving to become development vice president. He wanted my opinion of such a move. I offered my enthusiasm for how someone with his buoyant personality would be a successful fundraiser. But I thought to myself that he would probably become miserable later after he had lost the godlike status he enjoyed only to become someone people ran from when they saw him coming hat in hand.

He decided to accept another new challenge instead: head coach of the NFL's Los Angeles Rams. I'm sure the money was a bit better.

IV
Communicating with the Larger World

Where's the Fire?

To much of the Penn trustee, faculty and alumni family, *The New York Times* is sacred. Everyday the paper is scanned for citations, which are widely communicated to the campus. Other newspapers, magazines, and television are highly valued of course, but the *Times* is unique. Consequently, when I become VP for University Relations, one of my charges was to increase Penn's coverage.

The Metroliner became my office as I traveled to the Big Apple to court various individuals, foundations, and the media. I met with the *Times* editorial board to sing our praises and sent thank you notes upon each kindly citation. We invited all our alumni in the media to a champagne reception in the office Bruce Crawford, Chairman of the big advertising firm BBD&O. We were making progress. Then came the fire.

The fire was THE FIRE, that famous West Philadelphia inferno that was started by a Philadelphia Police Department bomb dropped on the roof of a barricaded and armed home occupied by a back to Africa group called MOVE. Mayor Wilson Goode authorized a police intervention, at the insistence of neighbors, to protect the many children in the building. Unhappily, the fire spread and dozens of homes were consumed in a debacle that still influences politics in the City of Brotherly Love.

The *Times* reported the fire on its first page. Unhappily, my success in raising Penn's profile backfired. The story included a map that had only two sites labeled: the fire and Penn. The scale was such that the disaster appeared to be virtually adjacent to our major dormitories. In fact, the fire was located about two miles from the Penn campus. Surely, our discomfort was minor compared to those of the neighborhood further west. Nonetheless, our switchboard was flooded with telephone calls from anxious parents expressing concern about their children. And future prospective student/parent visits had to explain and demonstrate that the campus was not located in the middle of a neighborhood about to go up in flames.

Then again, maybe the old public relations adage is valid, "All publicity is good publicity." Penn certainly became more visible to a national audience.

Explaining the Traumatized Apes

Treating head injuries is one of the most difficult and critical of emergency room activities. Athletic and recreational activity like football, motorcycles, and bicycles means that most head trauma effects young men and women. Accordingly, prevention through better head protective devices became an objective that elicited intensive research at our medical center. Unhappily, that research led to one of the more embarrassing incidents in our history.

A group of animal rights activists broke into Penn's head-trauma research-center over a holiday weekend, stole 60 hours of video tapes, and trashed the lab. The People for the Ethical Treatment of Animals (PETA) denied involvement, but the organization did facilitate the tapes appearing on national television. The images were very disturbing.

The experiments replicated an accident by rapidly accelerating a baboon's head so that the brain strikes the interior of the creatures' skull which causes fatal brain damage. Before the rapid movement is activated, the ape's head is encased in a plaster helmet. This plaster cast must be removed before the animal's brain can be autopsied and damage determined. Removing the plaster, however, involves chipping it away with a small hammer. All of these elements were gruesome to the average viewer. The baboons were quite appealing and human like; the rapid head movement with the animal's surprise, and the hammering of the plaster helmet all came across as sadistic.

Unhappily, some experimenters were smoking and making insensitive offensive jokes about the poor animals. It may have been the macabre humor that medical personnel often voice to put psychological distance between themselves and an unpleasant task, but laymen viewers found it deeply offensive.

Our initial response was to blame the weekend raiders as hooligans and criminals breaking into the building, stealing property and damaging medical equipment. This defense was a clear loser to the powerful disturbing images. Our second thought was to put the principal researcher, an eminent brain surgeon, in front of the camera to describe the benefits of the laboratory. Use reason and science to counter emotion – another losing approach. Complicating this strategy was that the messenger was at odds with the message. The physician was too assured, smooth and affluent appearing. His cultured accent, his expensive suit, gold cuff links and diamond tiepin just conveyed an elite disconnect with John Q. Public.

Our message only began to get through when we counterattacked with emotion. By recruiting head trauma victims who had been successfully treated with techniques developed at the Medical Center, we were able to develop videos, photographs, and texts that implied that the animal protectors were putting the value of the apes ahead of the potential needs of children and young adults

If a picture is worth a thousand words, a video multiplies the ratio by another factor.

What's in a Name?

Clear customer perception of a product or company is important. Marketing calls this "branding." And it is just an important to a university as to General Motors. For my university it has presented a challenge greater than for most schools.

The University of Pennsylvania is the formal name. It is a private institution founded by Benjamin Franklin with a vaguely "Quaker" association. Indeed, our sports teams feature a mascot of a Quaker in costume leading the oxymoronic "Fighting Quakers" football team. The university has been a member of the sports conference called "The Ivy League" since the league's founding in 1955. The term "Ivy League" has come to carry a wider association than just sports of course. The general public associates "Ivy" with some of the most prestigious and academically competitive schools in America.

It is important for student recruiting, that prospective students and their parents clearly see the University as part of the Ivy League. But our name has presented a problem here because The University of Pennsylvania sounds like a public state university. In contrast, our competitive rivals are almost always referred to without "university" attached: Harvard, Yale, Princeton, Brown, Cornell, Dartmouth. But, branding ourselves as just "Pennsylvania" presents other problems. It sounds like the state itself; or worse, it gets confused with Pennsylvania State University or "Penn State" which enjoys near universal brand recognition as a fine state university of great athletic renown.

When I was head of university relations, we made a firm commitment to push PENN as the label. We were betting that although sports devotees might be amused, the academic world would not confuse us with Penn State. We convinced eleven of Penn's twelve schools to feature a common logo on their stationery and publications: a large **PENN** at the top and, well below, a smaller "The Law School of the University of Pennsylvania," for example.

But one school didn't fit. It had a unique name: The Wharton School. The original name of what was the world's first business school was "The Wharton School of Finance and Commerce." Many years ago, in order to broaden its appeal, the name was shortened. But the name "Wharton" in the business world, and among many in the general public, was a stronger and more identifiable brand than the parent university's.

Some on my staff pushed me to pressure Wharton to subordinate itself to the PENN label. But that seemed unreasonable given what they had so successfully achieved with their brand. Indeed, as a long-time Wharton faculty member, I loved the brand. When former trustee Chairman Al Shoemaker was leading the creation of a university club in Manhattan, I suggested that we create a double brand name for the club by naming it **The Penn-Wharton Club**. I felt that would be attractive to both undergraduate and graduate alumni. But, this provoked a strongly negative reaction from non-Wharton alumni who tended to be skeptical of Wharton (by tradition, at graduation Arts and Sciences grads would, to the surprise of assembled parents, boo the business school graduates – supposedly for their single minded pursuit of Mammon).

I was happy with our compromise. Wharton agreed to stay close to the university type, color, and design of university materials with THE WHARTON SCHOOL in large letters and below it "The Wharton School of the University of Pennsylvania." Sure, it was a bit redundant, but the linkage was consistent.

Both sides thought I had sold out. My former Wharton colleagues thought I had been bought by the central university administration and my university relations staff thought I had compromised too much with my old school. A rose is not a rose by any other name.

I still cringe when Penn State football fans ask me if we are going to beat Ohio State next week We don't play them and PENN never will.

A Messy Medical Divorce

When I walked into the meeting everyone looked at me with a skeptical expression. I knew immediately what it was about. That morning the newspaper had reported on the defection of thirteen of the fourteen cardiologists at the Camden based Cooper University Medical Center. The meeting I was entering was a meeting of the Cooper Trustee Audit Committee on which I was then serving. The medical center that had stolen the physicians was the University of Pennsylvania. They had been recruited to set up a new cardiology practice in New Jersey. I was still employed by Penn.

No, I had nothing to do with the move and knew nothing of it in advance. Nonetheless, there was some wariness in the room as I participated in a most intimate discussion of Cooper's financial privacies. Some may have considered me a mole.

Like many divorces, the split of the Cooper cardiologists and their engagement to a new partner became messy. A central issue was a brand new building that the practice occupied in Cherry Hill, about ten miles from the hospital's location. Cooper claimed that they owned the building since the cardiologists had been its salaried employees. The departing cardiologists countered that that their practice had paid for the new facility so that it should go with them. Penn naturally supported their new associates.

A judge eventually became involved. After listening to hours of debate between the attorneys, he was reported to have exclaimed that he was tired of listening to rich millionaires arguing over who gets the dog and who the cat. Unless they reached agreement he was threatened to impose a Solomon-like judgment dividing the property as he thought fit.

A confidential settlement was reached, but quite soon, a large blue PENN signed replaced the maroon COOPER sign on route 70.

At times I worry about where the ambulance will take me if I should be found unconscious on a street near my home in New Jersey and in need of emergency cardio care.

Hors d'oeuvres at Tiffany's

Several times I was invited to give talks at the periodic colleges of the Young President's Organization. The YPO is an international organization of executives who were appointed Presidents of their businesses and non-profit organizations by the age of forty. They stage many learning opportunities culminating in regional and world colleges where they interact with eminent scholars and practitioners about business management and cultural developments.

One of the most memorable for me was held in New York City at the Waldorf Astoria Hotel. I conducted sessions on conflict and change management. On Saturday night, a gala cocktail party was held in Tiffany's on Fifth Avenue followed by dinner at the New York Botanical Gardens.

My wife was a vision of Holly Golightly that evening. The jewels on the YPO guests rivaled those in the Tiffany display cases. We chatted with assorted CEO's including one who had been a former student of mine. Another former student was the attending physician there to render medical assistant in case anyone slipped on a martini olive. At the appointed time, the crowd boarded their waiting bus for the trip north to the Botanical Gardens. Laughter and gaiety filled the bus as we proceeded north up Park Avenue toward the Bronx.

The hubbub began to decline, however, as the bus left the comfortable clime of the East 90's driving into the Harlem of the 100's. After we passed over the Harlem River into the then devastated South Bronx, all conversation died. The rapid wealth to poverty transition was just so dramatic. I (and perhaps others) conjured up the image from David Lean's film *Dr. Zhivago* of the bourgeois diners in the glamorous restaurant falling silent at the sounds of the red flag carrying would be revolutionists marching outside in the falling snow.

Yet we were in New York, not Moscow. And among the celebrants that evening was Mayor David Dinkins who was quick to point out to the guests the challenges confronting the City. And among the guests were entrepreneurs using to thinking in revolutionary terms about their businesses. And virtually everyone there cared deeply about New York City and wanted it to regain its preeminent place among American cities. Today that trip up Park Avenue still encounters many challenges, but the South Bronx is being transformed and New York City under its last three mayors Koch, Giuliani, and Bloomberg has witnessed a remarkable resurgence.

So much so that upon my retirement, I purchased an apartment on East 74th Street.

Fleeting Fame and Pain with Charlie Gibson

Andy Warhol overestimated the length of time that one can expect to be a media star. For me it was not fifteen minutes, but merely half of that based on an appearance on ABC's *Good Morning America* early in President Clinton's first term. I was to comment on Clinton's leadership crisis given the strongly negative response to his espousal of a tax increase and stronger rights for gays in the military.

As I was sitting in the Green Room awaiting makeup application (which I accepted; I had viewed the Nixon-Kennedy television debate), another guest was waiting to go on stage while cradling an orange tabby cat in his lap. He and his pet were to precede my appearance. I watched them on the green room monitor. What was their appearance about? Horror upon horrors, he had trained his feline companion to go potty on a toilet seat! Sure enough, this skill was soon demonstrated for the edification of morning viewers all over America. After a one-minute commercial break, I was introduced as an expert on executive leadership.

Well, I thought I was brilliant in replying to host Charlie Gibson's questions on the challenges facing President Clinton, but I did recall the old vaudeville warning: **never**

go on after a child or animal act! It's just too hard to get the audience's attention.

To make matters worse, as I departed West 60th in New York City in the luxurious limo that ABC provided to return me to the even more luxurious hotel in which they had put me up, I was stricken with the most remarkable pain in my back. As I lay in the hospital emergency room, a kindly nurse informed me that I was experiencing the greatest pain that male *homo sapiens* can incur – a kidney stone. She comfortingly observed that I would now know what it is like for a woman to give birth.

Happily, soon afterward an efficient young resident told me that she would give me an injection that would make me feel better than I had ever felt before. And she did. And I did. And the fame and pain quickly passed down the urinal -*sic transit gloria mundi.*

Good Morning America, Again

In spite of the pain associated with my first visit to ABC's *Good Morning America*, I accepted a second invitation to appear. This time I was luckier than I had been with the cat on the previous visit. Chita Rivera had just won a Tony for her role in *Kiss of the Spider Woman* so I got to chat with her in the green room (she brought her own make-up artist).

The 1990's economic boom was taking off. Business was expanding and demands on employees were increasing. Overtime work was at an all-time high and the work year in the United States consumed the most hours of any nation – even more than Japan and South Korea. The popular media was full of articles complaining about work related stress and the perils of burnout.

There was merit in these concerns and my interviewer clearly wanted me to validate them while casting blame on greedy employers. Nonetheless, I took a different tack. "Isn't it great?" I exclaimed: "How much better than the chronic underemployment of the 1970's and early 1980's. How great that we overcame the stagflation in our economy and that productivity was increasing at the fastest rate since the 1950's. Yes, Americans have the shortest vacations in the world (who wouldn't want a European-like five to six weeks compared with our average of 10-14 days?). Still, American work is driven by a national achievement need that goes a long way to explaining our relative wealth. Our willingness to work is one of the glories of the American character, etc., etc."

I guess I exaggerated a little, but I was enthusiastic.

Besides, global competition was increasing and we needed to work hard to maintain our position. Years later as a Director of a Dutch based engineering firm I had to explain to the European Employee Council why their retirement age was being increased and their paid holidays reduced, They feared that we were "Americanizing" the firm (with all the horror that <u>that</u> implies). No, I explained, the business world is simply bigger and more competitive. There were engineers in Romania and the Czech Republic (not to mention India or China) who could do much of their work. In fact, we were going to farm out work to them.

Recent calls in Europe to rollback work week decreases, postpone retirement, control holidays and introduce more employment flexibility, all testify to the wisdom in the United States of not idealistically reducing work expectations to impractical and insupportable levels.

All in all, I thought I was even better the second time on the show than the first. But, I was never invited for a third visit.

Rescuing Dale Carnegie

When the BIOGRAPHY Channel asked me to serve as a guest for their show on Dale Carnegie, his famous book How *to Win Friends and Influence People* was sneered at by most in my field. They considered its self-improvement thesis wishful thinking and hucksterism. Freud's unconscious, B.F. Skinner' behaviorism and psychological determinism dominated the way organizational psychologists conceived of the individual in organizations. And popular culture at the time called for everyone to be "natural" and "authentic"– to themselves. Carnegie's approach implied "acting" and "self-manipulation."

Of course, Carnegie oversimplified human behavior and thinking, but creative simplification is at the core of most successful leadership. And time is being kind to his simplification. The development of cognitive therapy and the psychology of optimism both suggest that whistling a happy tune can have a positive impact. There are ways of changing how one conceives and thinks about oneself and others that help in learning how to be more effective interpersonally. We all have flexibility limits, but new thinking and changed conditions can induce growth.

I was over forty years old and more than twelve years into my academic career before I even took a coffee break in the office to simply chat with whomever was also getting a cup. I was just so anxious to get back to my desk, usually to my writing. Of course I had to attend meetings and teach students, but ultimately, producing quality work requires the discipline to confront oneself alone with a pencil, paper, or computer. In writing multiple books and articles, I, like most academics, spent so much time alone that I became very self-centered. This is not criticism of myself or others. To produce valuable work, one must believe that what you are doing is critically important and that it should be protected from others' intrusions. Indeed, part of a university administrator's responsibilities is to create conditions that facilitate professorial self-centeredness.

My life changed when I moved into full time academic administration, human relationships became all encompassing and deeply satisfying. They provided the opportunity, so praised in most religious traditions, to transcend the self and beneficially touch others. Was it "natural" for me? Usually, but not always. I had to learn how to let go of myself and be more sensitive to others. Sometimes I had to act being "up," because when I behaved as if I were "down," much of my office would be down. And if they were optimistic and enthusiastic, I would quickly become so.

Dale would have been proud.

Palo Alto's Wonderful Aroma

1968 was a schizophrenic year. The horrible murders of Martin Luther King and Bobby Kennedy, the continuing Vietnam debacle, Johnson's withdrawal from the Presidential race, and the Democratic convention's riots followed by Richard Nixon's election as President dominate our shared memory.

In contrast, for the Webbers it was a wonderful year. We had built our first house, I published my first book, and together we spend much of the summer in California while I was teaching at Stanford. We all went to Yosemite, Muir Woods, and Disneyland. The contrasts were so dramatic.

Earlier I had been consulting in Albuquerque for the Sandia Corporation, designers of America's nuclear warheads. They were frantically looking to utilize their staff creativity and engineering know-how to design civilian products. On the flight back to Philadelphia, I stopped to meet with friends in Chicago. We shared a glorious meal in an even more glorious home on the north shore in Wilmette. The conversation turned to the stalemate in Vietnam for which the majority of the group, both men and women, had a solution: bomb the Vietcong back to the Stone Age with our nuclear weapons. I was stunned.

When I got to the Stanford campus in Palo Alto, I thought I had entered nirvana. The buildings and the weather were so beautiful. All about the campus were students lolling in the sun and throwing Frisbees. Yet, it soon became clear how conflicted so many of the students were by the war. Some wanted to escalate; more wanted the United States to withdraw. But all the men felt uneasy about luxuriating in heavenly Palo Alto while their peers were in Nam. The contrast was beyond comprehension.

As I walked with my wife and four children on a particularly lovely day with the sun filtering through a stand of Eucalyptus trees, I noticed a marvelous aroma which I attributed aloud to my family as coming from the trees, A student lying nearby with friends on the green lawn loudly corrected me, "No, man, that's my pot."

A new beast was slouching toward Philadelphia.

Shark Bites in Iceland

In the heyday of Icelandic Airways, the cheapest flight to Iceland's capital Reykjavik was through Luxembourg. One flew east from JFK International to Luxembourg City and then back west to Reykjavik. That was the route I took to talk to Iceland's assembled financial industrial and political elite. Unfortunately, the talk was on a morning after a forgettable meal with my hosts followed by a sleepless night of never setting sun and young kids playing soccer outside my hotel window.

When Americans visit a foreign culture, one's hosts frequently put you to the eating and drinking test. Do you have the guts to stomach what they present as their traditional custom (even if personally they reserve observance to only one annual holiday visit to the old homestead). So in Reykjavik I was presented with small tooth picked pieces of a grayish looking fish accompanied by a glass of innocent looking clear liquid. It was suggested that I put the whole piece of fish in my mouth, chew it, and then take a drink of the water appearing liquid. So I did, which quickly taught me why the drink was imperative.

The fish was aged shark. Apparently it had been buried somewhere for a year before becoming the delicacy that it was said to be. Eating it, however, produces an overwhelming rush of ammonia. It permeates the noses

217

and ears, which cry out for something, anything, to take away the taste. The anything is a clear liquid, aquavit-type liquor that works by almost killing its consumer. Ammonia and two hundred proof – what a pair.

The subliminal message coming from my fellow diners seemed to be that, for an American, I was a good sport to engage in this quaint torture. To be really accepted as *fjolskyda*, however, I needed to repeat the process. So I did, and it was easier than the first time. Indeed, I was beginning to think, what the hell, how about going for three? Fortunately, a kindly Penn alumnus who was a government finance minister suggested that it was late and I might need some sleep prior to tomorrow's talk.

I wish he had stayed around to shush those football players who were taking advantage of this land of the midnight sun. Never have I slept so well as on the return trip to New York.

Grappa or Scotch in Italy?

In the Alpine foothills north of Turin, Italy, FIAT had a lovely 18th century chateau that housed their mid-career executive development programs. For a number of years the Wharton School and FIAT's executive training group conducted a multiple week program that integrated classroom and at work research projects. Penn faculty would fly to Malpensa, the Milan airport (has there ever been a less reassuring airport name?), and then travel to Marentino for a week at a time to conduct sessions with the Italian mid-career managers, most with engineering training.

It was a long day that continued with a class after dinner. I was usually quite tired because I had difficulty adjusting my body clock and was awakened every morning about 4:00 A.M. local time by a very loud neighborhood farm's Piedmont cock. Adding to the challenge of that evening class was the Grappa I was pushed to drink by my students. I had never even heard of Grappa, but when told that it was an Italian Cognac, I really accepted the proffered glass. What a mistake.

As I was standing in the amphitheater pit facing the laughing group and struggling to regain control of my breath and tongue, I noticed that the liquid in their glasses was a different amber color. With near uniformity, they were drinking Scotch, neat. Grappa was reserved for the visiting rubes. Beware of Italians bearing gift drinks.

Both sides were very pleased with the program, but in time dramatic cultural differences emerged. The American professors had difficulty adjusting to the Red Brigade terrorism that was rampant. They were shooting the kneecaps of professors. We just couldn't understand why academics were considered important enough to justify such attention. We sometimes were escorted in cars preceded and led by machine gun toting Carabinieri.

In turn, the FIAT managers had difficulty understanding the mentality of American drivers. As we discussed FIAT's lack of success with United States sales, we explained that many loved the Pinin Farina styling but complained about unreliability and body rust. They, however, were incredulous upon learning that American owners themselves don't change their engine oil or brake pads. To so is a source of pride in Italy. And in fact, many Americans never ever even pay anyone to change their car's oil! In Italy, this is sacrilege; the students just couldn't believe it. And none of them had ever heard of spreading salt on winter roads. It just wasn't done in even Northern Italy. Body erosion was not an issue there.

The executive program operation was a success, but unfortunately, the patient died. FIAT ceased all U.S. marketing and retreated back to Europe. Beware of American professors offering advice.

La Regni Asparagi

American professors teaching in a foreign culture develop closer relationships than when at home. Competitiveness is replaced by cooperation. In Wharton's management development program with FIAT in Turin, Italy, three or four U.S. faculty at a time would teach alongside Italian colleagues for two weeks at a time. We became quite close.

Giorgio Inzerelli took me to visit his venerable mother in Milan where he introduced me to a killer concoction named a Negroni (which contains equal parts of gin, sweet vermouth and campari bitters). I will never forgive him. Carlo Sordi introduced my wife and me to the glories of the Asti Barolo vineyards. No complaint there.

This cross-cultural teaching sometimes highlighted cultural differences with respect to scheduling and time management. When we traveled to Turin for program planning, few meetings started with less than a twenty to thirty minute delay. And discussion never ended at a fixed time, only when the topic was completed. This usually meant no more than three meetings could be scheduled in a day.

It was dramatically different when the FIAT faculty came to Philadelphia. Every meeting started within five minutes of the scheduled time or the Americans present would begin to grow restive and resent late comers. Plus we worked on our hour and a half class schedule. So every meeting had a termination time that was 90 minutes after the scheduled start – whether or not the meeting topic was successfully completed. Our Italian guests found this very disconcerting.

When we were in Italy, during our limited free time the Americans would often explore the lovely Piedmont countryside looking for interesting restaurants. On one of our excursions in a rented Lancia Delta, we discovered a country restaurant named *La Regni Asparagi* (The King of Asparagus). It was a unique gastronomical experience. Every item on the menu was made from asparagus. The Cynar aperitif was followed by a crème of asparagus soup; then a white asparagus salad. The main course a roasted asparagus medley followed by asparagus soufflé. Dolce was sugared asparagus tips. Only the espresso was unthemed. It all tasted a lot better than it sounds.

For men (I don't know about woman), asparagus produces one of the strongest and longest lasting reminders of what has been consumed. Several times a day for a couple of days, every bathroom visit rekindles memories of the meal. Even today just eating a single asparagus serving reminds me of the faculty companionship on that Piedmont day. *Viva La Regni Asparagi!*

The Iranians Carry Their Own Bags

Meeting with Wharton's first director of executive education, I complemented him on the lovely Oriental rug that decorated his office. Yes, he said that he was very proud of it as it was a gift of the Shah, Reza Pahlavi. They had met in Iran during World War II and had maintained a relationship. In fact, the director had called me in to discuss a program for Iranian bankers that he had negotiated. They would be coming to Philadelphia for two weeks of classes, a visit to the Federal Reserve Bank and then Washington DC. He wanted me to organize and run the on campus portion of the program.

At the time, the school had no dedicated hotel or classrooms reserved for executive education participants. We had to scout around for available space. Prior experience suggested this could be chancy. I well remember the adamant complaints about the lack of air conditioning in our dorms voiced by a group of visiting executives from Nigeria. Not that I had much choice, but it hadn't occurred to me that Philadelphia in July would be hotter than West Africa. But then Philadelphia in July is probably hotter and more humid than anywhere in the world.

For the Iranian bankers we found space in International House in West Philadelphia, a rather austere monastery-like building used by foreign students, When the bankers arrived I should have recognized that we were in trouble. As they began to step out of their cabs resplendent in their Saville Row suits, Egyptian 400 thread shirts and Armani ties, they had so many bags and we had no baggage handlers. When I asked my director what to do, his response was a Marie Antoinette-like, "Let'm carry their own bags." Needless to day, they were not happy. One complained to me: "This is the first time in my life that I have ever had to carry my own bags!

Perhaps at that point I should have heard the far off rumble of the coming overthrown of the Shah and the Islamic Revolution.

On the Distractions of Bahamian Bikinis

Different venues have their unique attributes that interfere with holding an audience's attention. A YPO Executive Conference on Grand Bahama Island had more than its share.

The ballroom had a large chandelier that hung directly in the path of my slide projector's image. And no one could find out how to turn off the piped in Muzak. I felt like I was on the set of Lloyd Webber's *Phantom of the Opera*. Even my overconfidence in my speaking ability was not enough to overcome my concern that this one would be a flop.

A young president had the answer. Rather than a lecture, let's just talk about the topic, business ethics and social responsibility, informally outside next to the pool. It was a beautiful day so we did.

For a while we actually did discuss the pro's and cons of broadening the corporation's stakeholders to include the general public and long run social welfare by contributing to local, national and international needs. Echoes of Milton Friedman on the negative side and Clarence Walton on the positive filled the air. The heads of the smaller businesses generally sided with Friedman; the larger corporation heads argued for a broader and longer-term view. I began to notice, however, that many participants weren't participating and even among the active talkers, their eyes were not directed at me, or the other YPO'rs. Rather, their eyes were continually shifting sideways as if watching a tennis match. Only then did I realize what I was up against. Young women in attire appropriate to poolside in the Bahamas were walking back and forth behind me. Unfortunately, it would have been unseemly for me to turn around and join my students in their gazing.

Years later as I read of various business scandals, I would wonder if some of my participants got into trouble and were in jail because of the distractions on that day poolside at the Lucayan Beach Hotel.

Talking in Thailand

I often gave talks where I wasn't sure anyone really wanted to be there and was really listening. In Montreal I was inadvertently scheduled to give an after dinner talk on the opening night of the Stanley Cup hockey finals when the beloved Canadians were competing. I barely got through "Good Evening." In Cincinnati, I gave a similar talk to the local chapter of the National Credit Managers Association. No one left, but afterwards one attendee told me that my visit was a bit unnecessary because, "In Cincinnati, everyone pays cash."

Teaching executives in Thailand produced an even different experience – it was like being a character in a play written by someone else who hadn't given me a copy of the script.

I would pose questions in class but nothing spontaneous would occur. In case discussions, a participant apparently appointed in advance would answer with the collective position. Eliciting any other comments on the question was like pulling teeth. No individual wanted to say anything that would seem to disagree with the class conclusion.

I spoke in English which most seemed to understand, but at the end of each one hour class section, a Thai translation was given supposedly of what I had said. Actually, these translations were of my class plans, not of what actually was said. There was no flexibility.

Being accustomed to the debate in an American classroom, I discovered that everything on my agenda was covered by 11:00 am – and I still had four class hours facing me!

Only afterwards talking to the U.S. educated Chief Executive Officer did I gain insight into the situation. The CEO nicknamed Mickey was very comfortable with American style give and take. Besides, he saw me, the Wharton Professor, as a status equal. We were standing talking in the reception area outside the classroom. But no one else would join in. In fact no student (remember these were mid career managers) would even approach within ten feet or so. Although straining their ears to hear what we were talking about, the physical and status dimensions of power distance were so strong that no one wanted to risk a social *faux pas*.

All this would change in the evening when the students took me to dinner and Thai dancing. Here all social distinction was forgotten and conversation about work and life was congenial and free flowing, the traditional music mesmerizing, and the dancers as beautiful as any women I've ever seen. Unhappily, the next morning I was barely able to wake up and face another classroom day pulling teeth.

My stomach felt like it had swallowed the Thai sacred white elephant.

Fear of Losing Status Loses Status

During Lyndon Johnson's administration, I conducted numerous training sessions for U.S. Foreign Service personnel on cultural influences on management. It was heady stuff and I felt on top of the world. After one such day, I hurried to the D.C. airport to catch a small commuter plane back to Philadelphia. As the Fokker 24 aircraft bounced northward, we hit an unusually rough air pocket in which we dropped so quickly that the ice in our glasses literally hit the ceiling. After a moment of stunned silence, a fellow passenger exclaimed loudly, "Isn't this the glamorous life?"

So it is with the instability of status. The power of status distinctions to influence behavior hit me literally and figuratively with a jolt. When one of the Foreign Service sessions was over, three were leaving last: the young female Foreign Service Officer who organized the event, the Ambassador who was the host, and I. As we approached the door, I (in my obsolete gentlemanly manner) reached to open the door for the young woman; she reached to open the door for the higher status Ambassador; and he reached to open the door for me. The three of us collided in a crash at the door opening.

Status is important in the Foreign Service as it is in many companies where it can undermine morale and communications. For several years, Wharton conducted executive programs for FIAT in a lovely villa outside Turin, Italy. The students were the best and brightest of the firm's middle managers – mostly very fine engineers. For the conclusion of the six-week program, I wanted FIAT Chairman Giovanni Agnelli to talk to the group, invite questions, share lunch and be inspirational. Not only did Agnelli decline the invitation, but we never got any senior executive to accept. They just never seemed to have the time. The idea of standing in the classroom pit interacting with middle class employees was simply incomprehensible. As an Italian participant told me, FIAT's top management was like a black hole; "stuff goes in but nothing comes out." And as another added on the firm's class distinctions, "FIAT is the only company where you can be fired on Monday morning for picking up the wrong fork on Saturday night."

Contrast Agnelli with GE's former CEO Jack Welch. Welch attended a class with virtually every cohort at the Crotonville executive education center. He delighted in selling GE to GE, and in responding to the firm's future executives. His willingness to put himself on the line was a powerful example for General Electric executives.

So it is the same in academia. Unhappily, I was in attendance at a school faculty meeting when a university president appeared to announce the appointment of a new Dean. The president's background was in the humanities and he appeared to be visibly nervous in front of the business school faculty. He made his announcement and hurried off.

His unwillingness to invite questions was interpreted as either contempt or fear. In either case, his reputation with this group of faculty was instantly in tatters.

Professors as Corporate Court Jesters?

Business school, engineering and science professors have increasingly been asked to serve on corporate boards of directors. It is an attractive invitation promising contacts with eminent practitioners and substantial income. I served a cumulative total of almost forty years on four corporate boards and a large medical center. Most of the experience was compatible with my primary academic responsibilities, and enriched the content of my management classes. I was able to bring real life examples to my students including on occasion the in class presence of the managers involved in the cases.

The increasing demand on United States corporate directors brought by various scandals and the Sarbanes-Oxley bill along with new SEC regulations has certainly reduced the number of boards on which one should serve. And the risk has increased (as the unhappy story of the former Stanford Business School Dean who was Chairman of the Audit Committee for the ill-fated ENRON would suggest). Nonetheless, the interaction of academics and practitioners on corporate boards is desirable.

Still a professor on a board sometimes can feel like a king's court jester. When George Ball served as Undersecretary of State in the Lyndon Johnson administration, behind his back he was referred to as Lyndon's Jester because his repeated warnings about the Vietnam War were not taken seriously. Rather, his speaking truth allowed his Cabinet colleagues to feel good about themselves for supposedly listening to all sides. An academic can sometimes find himself or herself in a similar marginal status.

Many hardheaded business practitioners see academics as pointy-headed intellectuals, too theoretical, or worse, too idealistic (or as William Safire wrote for a Spiro Agnew speech, "nattering nabobs of negativism"). Warnings about the negative effects of downsizing will be heard, but attributed to the complainer being too soft. One's remarks will be heard cordially, but seldom with much weight. I once served on a European Supervisory Board along with an ordained minister and a Socialist Party leader (try to find that in the U.S.). They were highly respected as men, but seldom influenced substantive policy.

Strangely, I found my director's role often became one of psychological counselor to the Chief Executive Officer. Being at the top is lonely in the sense that one is limited in the candor that subordinates will offer. President Johnson became enveloped in a kind of velvet cocoon. And other CEO types on the Board just are too busy or too competitive to be of much help to a company President/Chairman feeling uncertain about relations with his or her board. I sometimes found myself becoming the lone "friend" on the Board. Being friendly with a CEO can be harmful to the firm and its shareholders of course if Board members become too dependent on the Chairman's good feelings that they censor what they do as directors.

Still, I take pride in the support and help that I gave some CEO's and Chairmen when they were experiencing personal stress. This support clearly was of more value than whatever I said at the Board meetings.

Even the boss needs a friend.

Outboxed at the Publishers' Book Show

I was excited to be asked to give a talk at the publishers' annual book show on Cape Cod. My first trade book, *Time is Money,* had been published by The Free Press and they had set up a display and rented a room for me to address the book sellers. My wife and I were especially happy to go because we had spent happy days there when newly married and I was serving in the U.S. Navy in Newport.

Walking into the convention hall, however, was just overwhelming. So many displays and so many books! For me it was stimulation overload. How could one possibly decide what to buy? And how would my modest tome (on which I had worked so hard) be even findable?

Well, of course, we were determined and we found the display table. And this rekindled my anger about a dispute that I had had with the publisher. I hated the title "Time is Money." It was a rip off from a Benjamin Franklin saying which I guess they thought appropriate given my connection with the university he had founded. But my title had been "Breaking Your Time Barrier" which I thought cleverer.

Alas, I discovered belatedly that my contract gave The Free Press marketing department control over the title, dust jacket, cover and title page design. Well, OK, if they thought that their borrowing from Ben would generate more sales.

I can't say that the hall was filled when I began my talk. But it wasn't embarrassing. And as at most conventions, people did wander in and out while I was speaking (thankfully, almost never done during a university class). As I spoke, I was pleased to see that some men were bringing in several cartons of books to be distributed gratis to the attendees. My pique with Free Press was dissipating as I admired their apparent marketing initiative.

Ending my talk, I graciously invited the audience to take a copy of the book as they departed. I refrained from offering to sign the books as I thought that would be too presumptuous. Luckily so, for I discovered that the books being picked up were not mine. Rather, they were of a competitor, Alan Lakein's *How to get Control of Your Life and Time.* Free Press had been outfoxed by Peter H. Wyden, a publisher of whom I had never even heard. My books were still in their boxes somewhere else.

I quickly recognized that *Time is Money* was not going to enable me to purchase a vacation home up the road in Chatham.

Inadvertently Defending Scientology

It was not intentional. I was asked to be an expert witness for the defense of a major Silicon Valley electronics firm against an employee lawsuit. The employee had sued because she claimed that a time management program required by her employer contained indoctrination into the teachings of the Church of Scientology. The attorney defending the firm asked me to evaluate the course materials and testify about my analysis.

When I read the course syllabus and its handouts, I was surprised to see that they did indeed contain materials written by L. Ron Hubbard, the founder of Scientology. But I detected no signs of religious indoctrination. Rather much of it was an old-fashioned repetition of the classical principles of management regarding chain of command, span of control, authority and responsibility, etc. The presentation was a bit old fashioned in a 1950's kind of way in that the author recognized no limits to his universality claim. He cited no situational or contingency factors for when bending the so-called principles might be justified.

The specifically time management portion of the course took a segmentation and focus approach. That is, recognize and separate one's job responsibilities, prioritize and focus on one task at a time. To reinforce the dangers of simultaneous multi-tasking, the participants were required to place multiple marbles on a plate and then maneuver the plate to allow one designated marble, and only that one, to fall off. It was indeed a difficult and embarrassing task for some participants. The employee plaintiff in this case may just have disliked this and other exercises. Still, nothing appeared to have an ulterior motive. And so I testified in my deposition.

But the Church of Scientology was involved. The firm's Director of Management Development had contracted with a company that was a wholly owned subsidiary of the Church. It was not established whether or not he was aware of this, but the consulting business appeared to be primarily a profit seeking operation. A confidential out of court settlement was reached shortly after I gave my testimony.

After reading later about the difficulties some people have experienced when in conflict with the Scientology, I am rather glad that I was an inadvertent witness for the defense – and on the winning side.

Bailing out of the Colonel's Foxhole

It was another expert witness experience. I was asked to assist the defense against a shareholder suit that claimed a regional bank had exercised poor judgment in making loans to "cronies." The loans were non-performing with a substantial possibility of being written off.

To assess the situation I conducted extensive interviews with mid level and senior managers including the President. The bank appeared to be a beautifully run. Certainly the buildings and files were immaculate. Response to depositors and customers was quick and attentive. Unlike some other banks that I had been in, strong leadership was clearly in place.

When I met the Colonel, I understood why. A retired Marine Corps officer, he was the long time bank president and Board of Director's chairman. Being an ex-navy man with three months of Marine Corps training, upon entering his office I almost came to attention and saluted. Large American and Marine Corps flags stood behind his desk. On it was his officer's sword along with assorted military memorabilia. He was most gracious and we shared some mutual war stories.

The Colonel was a legend in the bank and in town. Indeed he something of an institution in his civic support for the community. His personality was so strong that he dominated both inside and outside the bank. And this was the problem. His staff overwhelmingly admired him, but was reluctant to even look for weaknesses in the loan proposals he brought to them. Objections went unvoiced. And some of those proposals reflected his sense of loyalty to the community rather than their financial viability. He seemed to feel he could **will** his local friends to meet their obligations when they got into financial trouble. It was hometown banking of *A Wonderful Life* variety. He was Jimmy Stewart but also the war hero.

Perhaps unhappily, however, this banking by hunch, instinct and friendship was becoming obsolete. Or perhaps his judgment was just deteriorating. In any case, reluctantly I had to report to his defense attorney that my testimony would not help his case. A settlement was reached literally on the courthouse steps.

I didn't feel happy about not staying in the foxhole with the Colonel.

Hunting the Elusive Eureka

A great frustration for many management consultants is that they don't possess authority to implement their recommendations. After a report is made to the client, consultants are generally gone. Academics who moonlight in consulting are especially limited in their availability to follow up on implementation. Implementation, of course, often falls short of the consultant's aspirations or the client's unrealistic expectations. The consultant tends to blame the client for inept implementation.

Still, sometimes there are magical moments when one feels that even though an outsider without formal authority you have actually helped an organization to change for the better. Making this extra special for an academic is when it is shared with students acting as co-consultants.

I tried to involve students in my consulting projects. One of the most successful was with the Engineering Department of Philadelphia Electric Company. I was asked to address morale issues and assist in promoting better hierarchical communications. My surveys indicated that junior engineers were very dissatisfied. They complained of distrust, inadequate job challenge, and non-responsive managers. In contrast, senior engineers and supervisors expressed very positive feelings about the company and their work. Many viewed the unhappy junior staff as immature whiners.

A self-fulfilling prophecy existed. Supervisors didn't trust the juniors' work. So they withheld the more interesting and challenging technical tasks for themselves or overly checked the juniors' work nitpicking for errors.

I could have simply stated this, but probably with little impact. It is key to get managers to look at the situation in an analytical, non-emotional way. Working with my students, we selected a public case analogous to P.E. for discussion with the managers. The students role-played some of the unhappy juniors in the case. The eureka moment came when after some time criticizing the case complainers, a senior manager exclaimed aloud, "This is exactly like the morale problems we have here."

From that point on, we moved from the "other firm's" problem to "our" problem. And that was the beginning of departmental change.

For my participating students, one hopes it inculcated a taste for having an impact on real organizations.

May I Have Another Beer Please?

For five years, on behalf of Wharton Executive Education, I was traveling around the country conducting a two-day program in Executive Self-Management in various hotels and resorts. It was the first time in my career that I had been on an expensive account and housed in some nice facilities. The participants were mid and senior managers in business and not-for-profit organizations seeking help for managing the substantial burdens they carried as well as achieving better balance between professional and personal life.

Holding the participants' attention for twelve hours in class over two full days was not particularly challenging because, unlike undergraduates, they were intensely interested in the topic and I knew how to involve them in the discussing their personal experiences. The days, however, were exhausting for me. The participants had to pay attention only to me; I had to focus on the remarks of everyone who spoke and give a response good enough to move the conversation along. Worse of all, I would be on my feet the whole time moving around the room to stimulate involvement. My legs would really begin to ache. If I went out to dinner with participants, it generally meant more stimulating conversation leading to great difficulty relaxing and falling asleep at night. A drink was well anticipated by the end of the day.

On one my programs in New York City I was accompanied by my wife and five year son. They had a great time sightseeing in the city while I was performing my act. By the end of the second day, we were both pretty exhausted so we met in a restaurant for an early dinner and then the trip home. I enjoyed a beer so much I called for the waitress to bring me a second. At that, my wife in her fatigue became quite agitated. Perhaps worried about other drinking problems in the family tree or rightfully worried about the drive home, she audibly complained that I should not drink a second beer. Since the waitress was standing right at our table she became somewhat confused and advised us, "But, two beers aren't really too many!" Her wisdom has guided me ever since. After a particularly tiresome day, I would ask myself if it truly was a "two beer day."

Alas, as I climbed the academic ladder into senior administrative posts such days became more common. Except that vodka replaced the beer.

My Favorite United States Senators

I am a registered Democrat. It is an identification inculcated during boyhood. My father was a member of the International Brotherhood of Electrical Workers; my mother a 1920's southern liberal who graduated from the Atlanta High School for Girls. Plus I had earned degrees from Princeton and Columbia, Ivy League bastions of liberal faculty. Like religion, my political identification shaped my expectations when I finally got to Washington, DC as management consultant to the U.S. Senate Office Systems Research Project (a big label for designing the offices in the then pending third Senate office building, the Philip Hart building).

Actually meeting and working with twenty-one Senators upset some preconceptions. For me the Democrats had always been the good guys concerned about the common man and the Republicans suspect in their favoritism for the rich. What a surprise to discover that among Senate staffers there was near consensus that individually the Conservative Senators were nicer people than the Liberals were. They seemed to be in less of a hurry, more willing to take time to listen to staff and constituents. The liberals generally seemed too busy to be concerned about individuals in their zeal to help the masses.

Ronald Reagan's diary communicates great faith in the ability of individuals to help themselves and others. But this optimism is accompanied by less confidence in government's capability to help anyone. Repeatedly Reagan opposes liberal dream legislation, but he many times took personal time to order help to alleviate the plight of some modest person he had read about in the paper or heard about on television. His identification with individual cases of need is very touching.

I never met Reagan, but I did meet with the Senator whom Reagan chose to save his administration in its last days: Howard Baker, Republican of Tennessee. He was one of my two favorites. Politically he was not on the extreme right of the spectrum, but he was clearly a philosophical conservative (staring down on his desk was a large portrait of his father-in-law, the late conservative senator from Illinois, Everett Dirksen – it was a little frightening). Eying my past as an industrial engineer, Baker pleaded with me not to make the Senate more "efficient." He felt that it would be dangerous to speed up the process of drafting, debating and voting on legislation. It was the very deliberateness of the process that made the Senate the greatest deliberative body in the world. He wanted time to allow rational thought and self-interest to reach democratic compromises.

Unhappily, Baker's deliberative style did not translate well to national politics when he chose to run for the 1980 presidential nomination. Campaigning in New Hampshire he would response to questions with a thoughtful college professor like: "One the one hand, the proposal is…..; on the other hand, it …." To the media at least, he came across as indecisive and, worst of all, **dull**, **DULL.**

He was also tired because he was so conscientious that he was working a full day as majority leader in the Senate and then in the evening flying to New England to campaign.

What marked my other favorite Senator was that he was a rare liberal who was not running for President. Senator Abraham Ribicoff was a very senior Senator from Connecticut who told me that at nearly 80 years of age he no longer aspired to national office. Plus, his constituents now accepted that as a politician he was a wholesaler, not a retailer. He meant that unlike many of his younger colleagues he didn't solicit requests from individual constituents to which he could respond with vote gathering favors. Rather, he knew what was strategically important to Connecticut and he concentrated on these longer-term matters.

Ribicoff's priorities were absolutely clear and he communicated them repeatedly to this staff. Virtually every morning started with them gathered in his office with the floor open to any legislative assistant who wanted guidance on the Senator's thinking regarding current policy issues. No one feared incurring enmity by an embarrassing question. The mutual respect was most impressive.

How different was the atmosphere in one young Republican Senator's office (I shall leave him safely unidentified). His demeanor emphasized his higher status and discouraged thoughtful questions. He even had his desk on risers so that he would be seated higher than office visitors, hoping that it would put them at a power disadvantage. I felt like I was staring up at a Judge's high bench. Come to think of it, that's where he had started his political career.

Perhaps there is some merit in Benjamin Disraeli's famous dictum, as retold by Winston Churchill: "He who is not a liberal at age twenty has no heart. But he who is not a conservative at age forty, has no brains."

Now that I'm over seventy, I had better decide.

I Finally Meet Elizabeth Taylor

Yes, it's true. Those violet eyes are mesmerizing, especially when seen at a distance of less than two feet. It was not across a crowded room although the room was crowded. Rather, she was immediately in front of me waiting to be seated in the United States Senate Senators' Dining Room. She was there with her then husband Senator John Warner of Virginia. I was there as a guest of South Carolina's Senator Ernest Hollings while serving as a consultant to his Committee on Administration.

An iron rule of the Senators' Dining Room is that celebrity is not noticed and no one is given priority. We all waited in the queue. And of course I didn't ask for her autograph or gush about how I fell in love with her when she played Rebecca in the film Ivanhoe. I always took her side when we teenaged boys debated who was more beautiful: the Jewess Rebecca or the Saxon Rowena (played by Joan Fontaine). But I didn't tell her. Nonetheless, protocol was broken when an excited hostess singled her out for recognition and a breathless autograph request. Senator Warner, however, in his magisterial voice told Elizabeth that the request couldn't be honored. She smiled and batting those famous eyes, said, "Sorry."

For three years I commuted from my Penn office to Washington while working on the office design of the

Hart Senate Office Building. I worked with twenty-one senators whose existing offices were in the Russell and Dirksen buildings. All very exciting. Dressed in my grey pin striped suit, I would walk down the halls of the neo-classical Russell Building and hurrying aids would greet me, "Good morning Senator," even once "Good morning Senator Kennedy" (I had a lot more hair then – and Ted was a lot thinner), I began to think that this was the place for me! Then I realized that all the Senate aids seemed to be twenty-five years old. Anyone over forty must have looked like a Senator to them. An aging Senator Claiborne Pell of Rhode Island once complained to me that his overcommitted and impossible schedule was always planned by twenty-five years olds.

To demonstrate to the Senators what the Senate Office Systems Research Project was trying to create, the Capitol Architect constructed an office mockup in the park across from the Capitol Building. While there, I was told by one of the security guards, "If where we are standing in the park were a lake, fully half of the Senators would try walking across it on their way to the Senate chamber fully expecting not to get their feet wet."

Sounds pretty much like most tenured professors to me.

V. Leaving

To Teach or not to Teach?

Confucius once advised, "Find work that you love and you will never need to work again." In my academic career I certainly found work that I loved so why stop? Since compulsory retirement was eliminated, one really can't be forced out. So why retire? And I didn't, for a while.

An old cliché about teaching features a silver-haired Mr. Chips sitting on a raised stool in front of his class lecturing from a script to his enraptured pupils. It certainly doesn't pertain to a contemporary university class. I was in the pit of an amphitheater with students behind tables surrounding me on three sides. To keep their attention I had to stay on my feet continuously moving around the classroom to get in their faces and generate debate. For each class I had to carry hundreds of pages of handouts and overhead copies to be distributed to the students. And the classrooms were always in buildings other than where my office was located – and usually on a floor without an elevator. Surely, it was no country for old men.

In addition, I simply had to read the *New York Times, Wall Street Journal,* and *Philadelphia Inquirer* every morning before class. It would have been too embarrassing to be unaware of some relevant development. Although I truly love sports, when I began to read the sports pages first and procrastinate on the business section, I knew it was time to think about leaving.

Many evenings during my teaching career ended with me sitting up in bed reading student papers and memorizing the student bio-picture cards so I would be able to call on them by name on the morrow (students are insulted if you don't know their names – and I usually had almost 200 per semester). It just got harder to stay awake unless I turned on Johnny Carson or, later, David Letterman whom, thankfully, my wife also enjoyed.

Most fundamentally, I just couldn't force myself to read the critical professional journals. I could get through the popular like *Fortune* or *Business Week,* but the rigorous *Administrative Science Quarterly* became impossible. It was time to go.

Perhaps the student *coup de grace,* however, were the skeptical student comments about my teaching. As I had gained more visibility and some degree of renown as an academic leader, management consultant, corporate director and vice chairman, I would increasingly draw on these experiences to illustrate academic theories. To my surprise, some students on the confidential course questionnaires accused me of being a "name-dropping egocentric," and even "an egomaniac" for talking about my personal experiences. Perhaps I was turning into a boastful old man. I didn't think so, but maybe….

After moving to emeritus status, I taught part time in an evening program for working professionals for six years. The students were primarily technically trained scientists and engineers, many working for the region's health care and pharmaceutical industries. Some were reaching senior technical positions and wanted to develop themselves for managerial responsibilities. Working with them was one of my most satisfying teaching experiences. They were genuinely interested in the human dimensions of organizational life – certainly more than my previous undergraduate and MBA students who were focused on finance and numbers. They voiced none of the criticisms that my last MBA students had so I ended on a high note. The only drawback was that the format was a three hour class starting at 6:30 pm. I just couldn't summon the energy that vital teaching requires.

My father died at 66 after only a year of retirement. He never seemed to make the transition from his clock based work environment to retirement's open time. He had served for twenty five years in Master Control at the Columbia Broadcasting System headquarters in New York City. His job involved making sure that the right signals from around the world got to the proper stations and on the air at the correct time. It was a clock directed environment. The film about Edward R. Murrow, *Good Night and Good Luck*, accurately portrayed the controlled chaos of live broadcasting in the 1950's.

When he retired, Master Control's large sweep hand clock was removed and given to him (this was long before digital displays). I remember it on the wall in our home, but it no longer gave structure to his life. When he was still working, his great passion was fishing. From Long Island Sound, to Montauk on the Atlantic Ocean, to Tarpon Springs, Florida, seeking flounders, sea bass, tarpon or bonefish was the anecdote to his clock stressed life. But after retirement, fishing lost its allure. It was attractive only in juxtaposition to work. Undoubtedly, unknown to me at the time he was already ill when he retired. Nonetheless, the lesson for me was that I was not going to visualize retirement as a dramatic end of one's stressful life and the beginning of perfect leisure. Ideally, the transition should be gradual, a shifting of time priorities from vocation to serious avocation, an avocation started long before age 70, 65, or 62. When I "retired" at 72, I had already taken many fine arts courses at the Pennsylvania Academy of Fine Arts and been painting for thirty years.

In addition at age sixty five I had obtained a coveted golf membership at a Country Club. I enjoy it, but waiting until, retirement to learn how to play golf is not advisable. After eight years of trying I still haven't broken a 100.

During a certain time period in my life, I became the object of multiple searches for Deanships and Presidencies. It was certainly flattering and I enjoyed the recruiting visits and interviews. I always found Penn to be the more attractive institution. At one point, however, uncertain whether I should leave full time teaching and research, I consulted an older colleague who had become a Dean. He told me that it depended on whether

I wanted "to be," or "to do." In his opinion, as a school dean or president, one primarily is in a state of "being" that conveys status and power (however moderate it is in academia). But administrative demands make it very difficult to continue meaningful research, writing or teaching. It becomes too difficult "to do" anything. If "doing" is one's primary ambition, better to stay out of administration.

Fortunately, I ignored my colleague's advice and became a university vice president. As I look back on my time in senior management, however, It is not the power or status that I remember (although I was the only university official with an office wet bar!). Rather it is walking around the campus and seeing the buildings for which I raised money or seeing the displayed pictures of faculty members whose endowed chairs came from people I had cultivated. These live on.

Finally, Confucius was a bit misleading. If one finds work that you love, one can't stop. In my case, writing is an imperative that demands attention. And even if one doesn't call it "work," it is challenging and exhausting. When fully engaged, I wake up several times each night to jot down ideas in my bedside journal. I hope that you have found the fruits of some of that nighttime scribbling in this book to be enjoyable. If so, the sleeplessness has been well worth it.

Index

7563144R0

Made in the USA
Charleston, SC
18 March 2011